IMPERFECT HARMONY

ALSO BY STACY HORN

Unbelievable: Investigations into Ghosts, Poltergeists, Telepathy, and Other Unseen Phenomena from the Duke Parapsychology Laboratory

The Restless Sleep: Inside New York City's Cold Case Squad

Waiting for My Cats to Die: A Morbid Memoir

Cyberville: Clicks, Culture and the Creation of an Online Town

Imperfect

Harmony

Finding Happiness
Singing with Others

STACY HORN

ALGONQUIN BOOKS OF CHAPEL HILL   2013

Published by
Algonquin Books of Chapel Hill
Post Office Box 2225
Chapel Hill, North Carolina 27515-2225

a division of
Workman Publishing
225 Varick Street
New York, New York 10014

Printed in the United States of America.
Published simultaneously in Canada by Thomas Allen & Son Limited.
Design by Anne Winslow.

Library of Congress Cataloging-in-Publication Data
Horn, Stacy.
Imperfect harmony : finding happiness singing with others /
Stacy Horn.—First edition.
pages cm
Includes bibliographical references.
ISBN 978-1-61620-041-1
1. Choral Society (New York, N.Y.)   2. Choral singing—New York
(State)—New York.   3. Horn, Stacy.   I. Title.
ML28.N3C569 2013
782.5—dc23   2012051349

10 9 8 7 6 5 4 3 2 1
First Edition

In Memory of Frank Cedric Smith
Thank you, and Dilys, for the music

CONTENTS

I believe in singing. I believe in singing together.

—BRIAN ENO

IMPERFECT HARMONY

Anthracite is the most beautiful coal in the world. A coal car of anthracite emerging from the mines looks like a mountainful of dusty but sparkling black diamonds. It is also the hardest, densest, rarest, and most expensive coal in the world. When it burns, it burns blue, and if it catches fire underground it's almost impossible to put out. An anthracite fire that began in Centralia, Pennsylvania, in 1962 continues to burn today.

On the morning of June 5, 1919, in Wilkes-Barre, ninety-two men died in one of the worst disasters in the anthracite mines of Pennsylvania. It happened quickly. The men were riding in a line of mine cars when sparks from a trolley wire or a miner's lamp ignited twenty-four kegs of black blasting powder loaded in the rear. "There was a roar," read a newspaper account, "and in an instant every man and boy on the train was either dead or dying." Not long after that day, while scores of miners were still being treated for burns and amputated arms and legs, thirteen local men left their jobs in and around the mines and met at the Grant Street School, christened themselves the Orpheus Glee Club, and began to sing.

All the men in the Orpheus Glee Club were either miners or sons or brothers of miners. They also were mostly Welsh; for them, singing was how they celebrated and also how they grieved. James J. Davis, a Welshman who became the Secretary of Labor two years after the disaster, said in his autobiography, "I think the reason I have never cared for drink is this: the ease from mental pain that other men have sought in alcohol, I always found in song. . . . The whole land of Wales echoes with the folk songs of a people who sing because they must."

I know that need. I've been singing with the Choral Society of Grace Church in downtown New York since 1982. When I'm standing up there with the choir, looking out at a thousand faces glowing in the incandescent light, singing some of the greatest music humanity has ever produced, I believe I know what made those miners sing. It's true that I didn't climb up out of a coal mine, but I've lived half a century now and you don't live this long without knowing some of life's sorrows. As long as I'm singing, though, it's as if I'm inhabiting another reality. I become temporarily suspended in a world where everything bad is bearable, and everything good feels possible. "Don't cry. Sing," a man with family fighting in Afghanistan tweeted recently. I do both.

Singing invariably and exquisitely triumphs over all my

defenses; it has become a place where I still hope and still believe, and so I sometimes just lose it up there. I'll cry and cry with relief at the sheer joy of it all until vanity kicks in, when I realize my face must appear all twisted and funny because my lips are doing this weird quivering thing that I can't control. Can anyone in the audience see? *Wait, damnit. Where were we?* At that point I've realized that I lost my place in the music. *Damnit, damnit, damnit, damnit.*

The director of our choir has exquisite taste in music, but he also invariably picks pieces that are described as so challenging that they are either rarely performed or attempted only by the most professional choirs. We are not a professional choir. We are a volunteer community choir. So while I'm up there sobbing and thinking "life is wonderful," the rest of the choir is racing ahead, executing some ridiculously difficult run. I try not to panic, to not look like I'm panicking, but also to find a place to jump back in. Oh God, my nose is running. *Where the hell are we?*

In truth, I don't have a great voice. Those formidable runs we typically perform are especially demanding for me. But I practice night after night after night in order to keep up because I want to dwell in the world that singing reveals for as long and as often as I can.

This book is about that world and my almost thirty years with the Choral Society of Grace Church. It is also an eclectic history of group singing, conductors, pieces of music both famous and forgotten, the science of singing, and all the benefits that come from being in the middle of a song. Because for the past few decades, as boyfriends come and go, jobs come and go, cats live and die, a stay in a rehab when I was thirty, depression, broken engagements, and the deaths of those I love, there has always been this: The Choral Society of Grace Church. Once a week I return to one of the most beautiful churches in Manhattan, pick up whatever masterpiece we're currently working on, open my mouth, and sing. Life is hard, battles of all kinds continue to rage around us, and disappointments accumulate. But singing is the one thing in my life that never fails to take me to where disenchantment is almost nonexistent and feeling good is pretty much guaranteed.

A German Requiem

Written by Johannes Brahms during 1865–1868

**Performed by the Choral Society of Grace Church
most recently in the Spring, 2010**

To get to Grace Church, I walk east on Eleventh Street from Seventh Avenue to Broadway. It's a lovely walk that I've taken more than a thousand times. Some city streets are gray or brown, but this particular stretch is a magical mystery tour of color, even at twilight. Nature and humanity have had a couple hundred years to settle into a luscious coexistence on these four blocks, and it's like walking through a friendly forest that has been peacefully settled by people. In the spring and summer, boxes of brilliant flowers and strange plants crowd almost every apartment window, some with leaves so large they look tropical. Clover, wood-sorrel, crab grass, and violets sprout from the sidewalk cracks that are off to the side, and there's always a sweet perfume that comes from either wisteria, pine, or honeysuckle. Steam rises from the manholes like water escaping from a pot. Branches from each side of the street reach across, forming awnings overhead whose leaves sound like hundreds of tiny drums whenever it rains. In the winter, holiday decorations pick up where nature leaves off and the color comes from tasteful wreaths hanging on the windows and doors, and garlands of pine and Christmas lights winding down the wrought iron gates, railings, and balustrades.

Rehearsals are every Tuesday evening from 7:15 to 9:30, so this is a walk I take at night, when my view is lit by the moon, street lamps, and whatever light filters out from the first-floor parlor windows. It's a very wealthy part of town and it shows. Sometimes I feel like the Little Match Girl as I pass by, forever on the outside, catching glimpses through lace curtains of the enchanting lives in these small palaces of glimmering chandeliers, floor-to-ceiling bookcases, and grand pianos. In one window is a small, sad painting of a gerbil with lettering that reads: In memory of Mr. Pokey, 2001–2003. In another is Paddington Bear. For as long as I can remember that bear has stood in the window, looking out, his outfit regularly changing with the seasons. It's the beginning of January now, and he's dressed in a top hat and tails, as if he's been making the holiday party rounds.

As I make my way east, it's as though a small storm has been raised whenever I hit the avenues that run perpendicular to Eleventh Street. In New York City, the cross streets are mostly residential and therefore quiet, while the avenues are commercial and loud. Crossing the thoroughfare, it suddenly becomes brighter and noisier with taxis and buses and bicycles and people. And then, just as suddenly, it's back to the protected calm of Eleventh Street. The last two blocks before I get to Grace Church are filled with antiques shops. I've never once stopped inside any of them, and I probably never will. The splendid gilded tables and French country armoires are much too grand for me. The very last block is relatively barren, the vegetation tapers off, and a parking garage takes up almost a third of the south side of the street. And then I come to Broadway.

Every time I turn that corner and look up at Grace Church, I'm no longer the Little Match Girl; instead I feel like Dorothy when she first steps out of her colorless Kansas farmhouse and into the land of Oz. The evening light hits the windows, spires, and tower of the church and makes it glow. When Walt Whitman came upon the same view, he described Broadway as a sea and Grace Church a "ghostly lighthouse." For me, it's a building that casts a spell, beckoning all to come inside to join the bewitched.

"PLACES, PLACES," JOHN calls out a few minutes before 7:15. We always begin exactly on time, and the one and only time choir rehearsal was ever canceled was on 9/11. John Maclay is the third director of the Choral Society of Grace Church. When organist and choirmaster Frank Smith retired in 1992, he was succeeded by Bruce McInnes, who retired in 1999. Of the three choir directors I have now sung under, John is the most obsessive and meticulous. He regularly distributes handouts with incredibly minute and fussy directions like, "Diphthongs are two vowels in one. Always give precedence to the first vowel, adding the second at the last possible moment." And then he gives a precise and phonetically spelled-out example: "house = HAAAAH-oos." He used to type up and print out stickers for everyone to put on the front of their music listing their name, telephone number, key dates for the rehearsals, his number and e-mail, but then he stopped. My theory is that some choir member affixed the sticker to his music folder crookedly and that one askew sticker taunted John for the rest of the season.

But John's perfectionism is why a reviewer once wrote of us, "I assumed that this would be a pleasing concert, although an amateur one. I was wrong. It was magnificent." The reviewer had been going to a lot of holiday concerts that month, "but none has been even close to the level of professionalism of this strictly volunteer group." He talked about our discipline and passion and then said we were "amateurs in the best of all possible senses." That is all John. John and his insane attention to detail, a devotion that I'm guessing keeps him up long into the night, looking for yet another way to make us hear and appreciate some impossibly subtle nuance in whatever piece we're working on. "Wake up and listen to the intervals around you," he called out to us recently.

The conductor sets the tone. It's his job to determine what the composer wanted to express and then elicit that from us, by any means necessary. You need a powerful personality up there, but not an egomaniac. If the conductor is too narcissistic, it's painful for the choir. Self-involved conductors will talk and talk and talk, usually about themselves. *Yeah, yeah, you're great. Can we sing now?* John goes almost too far in the other direction. It's only about the music for him. Until recently all I knew about him was that he's a lawyer, and while he was in law school he was the assistant conductor of the Harvard Glee Club, but that was about it. John has another quality that compounds the mystery. When he's up there on the conductor's platform, directing the choir, we're mesmerized. Whether he's directing our singing, telling us gossipy stories about the composers, or giving us impassioned explanations about what music means and what the composer was trying to communicate, he has our rapt attention. John has a tremendous ability to convey his enthusiasm from that protected perch, and whatever he tells us, we believe him. He always manages to take the shared pleasure of singing and amplify it. We'd miss a lot of beauty if it weren't for John Maclay. He is a substantial, commanding, and charismatic presence, from a distance.

Up close he's more restrained. He's perfectly friendly, but somehow conversations with John are always over in seconds. It could be that he's just shy. So while I can describe what he looks like up there on his stand—light hair, light eyes, a trim, handsome, youthful-looking fortyish man, always dressed in crisp, pressed white shirts—for the most part John Maclay remains an enigma.

When I asked my fellow choir members for impressions

of John, soprano Christina Davis was one of the people who responded. "I remember a bunch of women in the choir each sharing the moment when they first realized John was gay. It was always a very Greenwich Village rite of passage, given his elegant 1920s-style good looks and Cantabrigian intellectual brilliance to realize he was not likely to be interested in you. But, in some ways it helped to remove any romanticism (at least on a heterosexual woman's part) from one's reverence of him."

"TAKE YOUR SEATS," John calls outs, less patiently now, and I start to look around for a spot. Rehearsals take place either in the church itself or in the Grace Church School gym. Tonight we're practicing in the church, where we have a choice of sitting in pews in the front or on plastic chairs farther back. Finding a seat of any kind, however, has become a delicate and sometimes dangerously fraught operation. Once, two sopranos tried to tell my friend and fellow soprano Barbara Sacharow and me to move from the seats we had taken in a pew. "We saved these seats," they insisted. But saving seats was not done back then, and while they actually had left a couple of their belongings behind to mark their territory, I thought they were items forgotten from a service earlier in the day. I started to explain, but they didn't give me a chance. "Move," they demanded, their faces hovering above us, angry and accusing, never once considering that it was an honest misunderstanding. They were so off-putting about it that Barbara and I both refused. The following season a tenor muttered, "Bitch," when one of them walked by. I looked at him with a mix of surprise and pleasure. "Oh yeah," he said. "I hate her." Small victory.

Emma Berry, an alto, who chose our choir because it met on the right night and in the right location, tells the story of taking a seat nearest to the restrooms when she was pregnant. A tenor quickly approached her. "I sit here usually." "Uh-huh," she answered. "No really. This is where I usually sit." "Listen," she explained. "I'm sitting here because it's near the exit and I need to be here so I can go to the bathroom easily, which I need to do about every thirty seconds." "Oh for crying out loud," he said before stomping off. The person next to Emma roared with laughter, but it's true that people tend to sit in the same seats and if you show up and your regular seat is taken you feel momentarily lost.

My favorite spot is in the pews that were built specifically for the choir in 1903, where I hurry now to grab a seat. For over a century, thousands of singers have sat here, singing many of the same pieces we sing now, feeling many of the same emotions. I love taking my place in history even though that also means being surrounded by reminders that just about everything is more permanent than I am, than all of us. There's a lovely carved wooden chair next to the pew where I sit. On it is a plaque that says that the chair was put there in 1892 by someone named Julia P. Fisher (in memory of an unnamed dead sister, I later learned). No one I know remembers Julia or her sister. But it must have been a cherished spot for her, too. One hundred years from now, others will be sitting in this pew, next to that chair, probably singing the same works I'm singing and looking around just as I am now. How many of them will take a moment to think back to the living, breathing, happy chorister who used to sing here? How many will think of Julia or her sister or me?

My preferred place secured, I wait to see who's going to sit next to me and behind me. It matters. Those are the people you can hear, and a flat singer will pull you down, spoiling the fun, while a great singer with perfect pitch will pull you up, making you sound better than you would have otherwise. I look around. The evil duo is nowhere in sight. I hope that Barbara will get here in time to sit near me (I still have mixed feelings about saving seats). She has a lovely voice, and she can sight sing. Barbara can pick up a piece of music she's never seen before and sing it as if she's been singing it her whole life. I can't do that. Basically, Barbara is the kid in class whose tests I've been cheating off at every opportunity. Barbara joined the choir because her marriage had broken up and she "needed to find something just for me." She'd sung in choirs through high school, college, and graduate school, and "when I thought what my life was missing most, it came down to music." She worried that she'd be "the only Jew singing about Jesus," but quickly discovered that beliefs and faith within the choir were all over the religious/nonreligious map. A lot of people join after recognizing a sense of something missing in their lives, it turns out. Christina Davis told me she became a member as a result of two events, 9/11 and turning thirty. Both caused her to look at all that she had sacrificed in her life, and "Foremost among these losses was choral singing."

Unfortunately, Barbara is nowhere to be seen. She works as a library teacher at the Fieldston School in the Bronx, and she has to run home, have dinner, check her e-mail, and grab her water bottle before heading for choir and frequently arrives minutes before we begin.

At the moment, to my immediate right is a soprano who doesn't seem to like me and who is making a point of not talking to me while we wait for everyone to get settled. I look around for people I know. Even after all these years, I don't want to sit here not talking to anyone, looking like I have no friends. I pick up John's most recent handout and start reading to camouflage my anxiety. Then Caroline, a new soprano, sits to my left. She has a pretty voice and she's nice. Then two friends sit in front of me. I start to relax and feel happy that I'm here.

After a brief warm-up we open the piece we're going to perform in April, *A German Requiem,* by Johannes Brahms. Although I've done this piece twice before, it's in German and I no longer remember what the words mean. Just because this is church music, one shouldn't assume it's about something . . . churchy. One Christmas we sang a piece by the British composer Benjamin Britten that referred to a few missing children. "Timothy, Mark, and John are gone, are gone, are gone, are gone, are gone," one line went. Turns out that one particularly hard winter the boys were butchered Sweeney Todd–style and salted down to eat. "Famine tracks us down the lanes, Hunger holds our horses' reins." We were singing about cannibalism. Cannibalizing children, no less. I looked out at the audience when we came to that part. Are they getting this? The actual text of the piece might be vague, but the title is *Nicolas and the Pickled Boys* and it's printed right there in the program. The chorus ends with St. Nicolas bringing the boys back to life ("Timothy, Mark, and John, put your fleshly garments on!") who then sing "alleluia." For the performance, we had three choir boys who walked down the center aisle of the church, singing in their pure and innocent voices, without a hint of the grisly deaths they'd just suffered.

John tells us to pull out our pencils and get ready to start marking our music with his directions. "If you don't have a pencil, mime the act of having a pencil." We begin. Something is up with John tonight. I didn't think it was possible for him to be more of a perfectionist, but he is having us repeat small sections over and over until he gets it where he wants it. We never quite achieve the sound he wants. "More *sostenuto*!" More this! More that! "Draw the sound out, don't push it out!" He tries having each section sing it alone, first the tenors, then the basses, the altos, the sopranos. But he is not satisfied.

There's a soprano in the pew in front of me who keeps whipping her head around to scan our row. I immediately think someone sounds bad and she's trying to figure out

who. *Is it me?* She keeps turning around. *She is looking at me!*
Seconds later most of the sopranos make the same mistake.
Everyone leans forward as one to mark the spot with our pencils. If you watched our rehearsals from above you'd see waves
moving throughout the chorus, as everyone bends forward
and back to mark their scores. Sometimes I make a show of
marking the spot where I've made a mistake in order to signal
to all around me (the soprano in the next row, for instance)
that, yeah, I know I messed up and I'm going to go back later
and learn it. *See? I get it.*

In only an hour my score is filled with marks. Not all of them
are about mistakes or John's directions. I've made a practice of
scribbling in asterisks next to my favorite parts in the music. I
put them there because I don't always remember where they are.
They're like small signs that remind me, "Bliss Ahead!" I know
that as long as the world doesn't end in the next few seconds
something very good is about to happen to me.

"The wonderful thing about the amateur chorus," the conductor Robert Shaw once said, "is that nobody can buy its attendance at rehearsals, or the sweat, eyestrain and fatigue that
go along with the glow; and nobody but the most purposive
and creative of music minds—from Bach in both directions—
can invite and sustain its devotion."

That's because it gets you out of the house every week to do
something that is like exercising joy. As I move firmly and in-
exorably into midlife, I need it more than ever. I thought that
these would be the easy years. I was sure I'd be settled by now,

not wondering how I'm going to pay for all the dental work I just learned I needed or still crying about the last guy who broke my heart. Last week I read an article about an experimental treatment developed by researchers at the Dana-Farber Cancer Institute/Harvard Medical School that reversed aging in mice. "Hurry scientists, hurry," I thought when I finished it. I need more time to get my life together.

Walking home tonight after the rehearsal, however, after a night of singing about death, I feel happy. Although George Bernard Shaw once described the Brahms *Requiem* as something that "could only have come from the establishment of a first-class undertaker," I don't feel in the least bit gloomy. I love his *Requiem*. Everyone in the choir does. Tonight John explained one of the reasons why. For much of his life, Brahms was a choral conductor. In his requiem there are all sorts of obvious clues that Brahms must have had enormous affection for choirs, but one big tip-off, making this choral work a choir's dream come true: the Brahms *Requiem* has relatively few solos.

Here is what performances are like for the choir: getting to sing, and then waiting as patiently as we can for the intervening solos to end. For the whole performance it's sing, wait the solos out, and then phew, we're finally back to the only part we truly care about, us singing again. If it were up to the choir, solos would be greatly shortened or eliminated entirely. There are exceptions, and if the soloists are brilliant it's not quite so tedious a wait, but for the most part solos are a barely tolerated side-trip while we wait for the good parts. Us.

There's another reason why singing his requiem feels so good. There is some debate about the religious views of Brahms. *A German Requiem* is relatively free of Christian dogma; instead of employing the standard Latin Roman Catholic requiem mass used in other requiems before and since, Brahms picked and chose his text from the German Luther Bible. When asked, he specifically declined to add lyrics referring to "the redeeming death of the Lord." Brahms biographer Jan Swafford writes, "He fashioned an inwardly spiritual work, full of echoes of religious music going back hundreds of years, yet there is no bowing to the altar or smell of incense in it." Although the Lord is still all over the place in the text, *A German Requiem* is about feeling better. Unlike most requiems, Brahms wrote his for the living, not the dead. "Blessed are they that mourn," it begins, "for they shall be comforted." The composer Antonín Dvořák once wrote about Brahms, "such a fine soul— and he believes in nothing!" But it's not as if God were our only option.

"Music idealizes emotions negative and positive alike," Robert Jourdain writes in his book, *Music, the Brain, and Ecstasy,* explaining why singing is beloved of coal miners, middle-aged city women, and countless others. And, "by imparting pleasure even to negative emotions, music serves to justify sufferings large and small, assuring us that it has not all been for nothing." In other words: life is hard, singing is heartening. And singing with other people, in particular. Those coal miners weren't singing to hear their own voices, they were singing together to know that they didn't have to face this miserable life alone and it wasn't all just misery. In times of sorrow (and celebration) there are two other things to believe in: music and each other.

This is a world where a song about death can give birth to great happiness. Alto Missy Backus told me about her first year at college. "I was very depressed and socially isolated and I joined the university symphonic choir. The rehearsals were one of the only bright spots in my week—they provided me with a sense of community and I enjoyed feeling surrounded by others who shared a love of music and performance. My first semester, we performed the Brahms *Requiem*. It was one of the only times I have been moved to the point of tears while performing; it gives me chills even now to think about it.

"Several years later, I started dating a guy named David and shared with him how meaningful the Brahms *Requiem* was to me, and how it provided me with comfort during a particularly dark period of my life. He surprised me with tickets to a performance of the *Requiem* at Carnegie Hall in January 2005. I married David in 2009 and he attended our performance of the *Requiem* in spring 2010."

John once e-mailed the whole choir about requiems in general. "The passage of a life, as no other event, causes human beings—and humanity generally—to reflect on life and the nature of the human spirit as no other event. There is nothing more primal, more communal, than the death rite. It is universal to all times, all cultures. It is equal parts sorrow for the departed, relief that we are still here, a more general celebration of the human spirit and a reminder of our common bond. To the extent that art is a distillation of life and the human spirit (and I believe that it must be), a Requiem cannot fail to motivate the best of the best—often at the worst of times."

The Verdi *Requiem,* he told us, was sung by the prisoners at Theresienstadt (Terezin). "Through the course of a single year, the concentration camp was alive with the Verdi, learning it by rote, and singing it numerous times for their torturers. The membership of the choir was replaced four times during that year, but they persisted, and etched out an indelible example of the power of art and the human spirit."

EVERY TUESDAY NIGHT a hundred people or more gather together in Grace Church. We'll say hello, tuck our bags and brief cases underneath our seats, warm up for a bit, and for the next two hours, sing. It doesn't matter if we're stumbling through something we're attempting for the first time or perfecting pieces we've been working on for months, it will feel great. You can't reach heights like this singing alone in the shower. As I walk back down Eleventh Street toward home and my cats, I can't stop singing one of the lines John made a point of translating: *kommen mit Freuden.* "Come with joy." I'm one day poorer, another day singler, and we're all going to die, but together with all these people I have raised my voice and once more I have come with joy.

The Orpheus Glee Club

A couple of years after the 1919 Wilkes-Barre mining disaster, James J. Davis, then Secretary of Labor, came up with an idea for a Federal Bureau of Recreation. "Existence without music," he said, "is a drab, drear thing for an individual or a people. . . . We, in America, could take no single step that would advance our nation along the road to happiness further than the establishment of a national means of exercising the power of music.

"I would teach music to everyone. Not merely the technical reading of musical notes, or the mechanical manipulation of an instrument, but the true meaning behind the music. We may all listen to the great masterpieces played or sung and know that the playing or singing is great, but how much greater is the enjoyment which comes of knowing the story, of love and life, or sorrow and tragedy, that was in the mind of the composer. . . . Words that tell an emotional story, set to appropriate music, burn into the soul."

As wonderful and noble as his idea was, the Federal Bureau of Recreation, as Davis envisioned it, never happened. I can't help regretting the missed opportunity. In the years since, as a nation we've gone from regular, active participation in music making to merely listening. I'm not talking about being in a choir, which is a serious, committed activity. But the kind of singing that used to be part of everyday life. When people would routinely gather around the piano in their homes and sing. Or they'd get together to play the banjo or fiddle and other instruments and sing old-time folk songs and dance. It wasn't about having a great voice or performing. It was just a fun thing people did for themselves or each other. As budgets are cut, however, music has been slowly disappearing from our schools. We've become accustomed to our passive role as the audience, many thinking we don't even have what it takes to sing. While the joy and solace of listening to great music are undeniable, today relatively few know the kind of passion that would inspire someone to write about music that can "burn into the soul," or the supreme comfort that would rouse a group of miners to transcend the sight of the smoldering remains of their comrades and emerge from the mouth of hell and sing.

THE CONDUCTOR OF the Orpheus Glee Club was a Welshman named Gwilym Amos who worked for the Lehigh and Wilkes-Barre Coal Company. His father, William, also a miner, had been slowly dismembered, piece by piece, by the mines. First he was badly burned in a mine fire. Then one of his arms was cut off when he fell under a coal car. When they gave him a safer position as a door tender, where his only task was to open and close the mine door, he had yet another accident and lost a leg. Later, in one more injury, he lost an eye. But his son Gwilym fared better. He got an education and a job in the front office.

Within a year of forming, the Orpheus Glee Club had grown to fifty singers. It wasn't long before they were itching to do what singers in Wales do: compete at an eisteddfod (pronounced eye-STETH-vode). An eisteddfod is a Welsh competitive festival celebrating singing and literature, and the first to be held in America was in Pennsylvania, in 1850. But was the Glee Club ready to compete with more seasoned, established choirs after only one year?

Gwilym Amos's conducting technique was far from the more flamboyant style you often see today. He guided his singers by facial expressions and the smallest of hand gestures, and his manner was so subtle and subdued that people in the audience would later claim that they never saw him move. But in his quiet way Amos was very demanding, always insisting on precise attacks and release, and, according to an article in the local Welsh newspaper, "good tone quality at all times." He was particularly strict about attendance, and the Glee Club's weekly average was an unfathomable 97 percent.

To beat attendance records like that you'd have to form the "Show Up and We'll Give You a Million Bucks" glee club. Whatever Amos was doing, it worked. The Orpheus Glee Club won the very first singing competition they entered, at the Philadelphia Eisteddfod in 1920. They kept competing and they won in 1921, 1922, 1923, 1924, and 1925.

Their triumphs only heightened their musical aspirations, and the men in the Orpheus Glee Club soon yearned to test their mettle in the motherland, at the greatest contest of all, The Royal National Eisteddfod of Wales. But Gwilym Amos fell ill that year, and a miner's strike the following year dashed the men's hopes of raising the money they needed for the trip. They never made it. On November 19, 1928, a windstorm swept through Wilkes-Barre. Amos was rushed to the hospital when the shanty he'd run to for cover was demolished by the storm. Two months later he retired from the mining company and the Orpheus Glee Club. Less than six months after that he was dead.

The Orpheus Glee Club sang on following Gwilym Amos's death, occasionally winning prizes, and in 1952 they changed their name to the Orpheus Choral Society and started admitting women. Today the thirty members of the Orpheus Choral Society rehearse on Tuesday evenings at the Firwood United Methodist Church in South Wilkes-Barre. They sing show tunes, as well as popular and sacred music, and compete in an eisteddfod at the Dr. Edwards Memorial Congregational Church in Edwardsville, Pennsylvania, every spring.

The Chichester Psalms

Written by Leonard Bernstein in 1965

Performed by the Choral Society of Grace Church
in the Winter, 2009

If singing in a choir has taught me anything, it's that what may initially seem strange and dissonant can later strike some of the most harmonious chords in your life. At 7:15 on the dot, we started working on what was to be our showcase piece that winter: Leonard Bernstein's *Chichester Psalms*. Fifteen minutes into rehearsal I decided that the seemingly sweet, wonderful, Young People's Concerts–conducting, *West Side Story*–writing Leonard Bernstein must have hated us. The same guy who was so beloved that New York City construction workers removed their hard hats and said, "Good-bye, Lenny," when his funeral procession drove by. That's because those construction workers never had to sing his *Chichester Psalms*. Jesus Christ. How are we supposed to count this? It's in seven. Is that even rhythmically allowed? Imagine tapping your foot to something you're listening to. It's usually going to be a beat like one-two, one-two, or the waltz's one-two-three, one-two-three. Now imagine counting one-two-three-four-five-six-seven. It's just weird. (By the end of the piece we'd be singing in ten.) I Googled the *Psalms* later and wasn't surprised to read that they were "noted among performers for their musical difficulty." My friend Barbara told me that the *Chichester Psalms* are in seven because of the sacred nature of seven in Hebrew. *Great. They couldn't revere four?*

At the beginning of rehearsal John had passed around a single sheet of paper. On one side was the schedule for rehearsals and on the other were our singing assignments. I'd been singing the same part for the past twenty-six years, so I hadn't looked down at the sheet in my hand. Until now. I was still reeling with rhythmic confusion from *The Chichester Psalms* and at first I couldn't find my name. Then I spotted it and almost threw up. I remember it got really bright for a few seconds, then dark—like a pre-passing-out response. I've been a soprano 1 for my entire choral life. That's the part that sings the highest notes, the best notes, and the best part of the best notes: the melody. I loved being a soprano 1. It also made me feel proud. I was on top. Number one. But when I finally found my name it was under the column for sopranos 2s, the part that sings beneath the soprano 1s. I'd been demoted.

I couldn't breathe. I had no time to recover and focus before John raised his baton and expected us to start singing.

I could barely read my music. It took me a few moments to find the stupid soprano 2 part in the score. Then I struggled. I couldn't figure out how to find my starting note. Instead of easily going to the one floating high above everyone else in the choir, I had to find some lesser note underneath. It was like trying to pluck notes out of thin air. I'd try and try, but every note out of my mouth was so wrong it sounded more like croaking than singing. I was miserable and I was making everyone around me miserable. Hitting an incorrect note causes the vocal equivalent of a car crash. Your wrong note throws off the people next to you, which throws off the people next to them, and so on. I was causing twenty-car/voice pile-ups repeatedly, and people kept shooting me glances. "I'm sorry, I'm sorry, I'm sorry," I whispered.

I couldn't bear it. We weren't supposed to raise issues of this kind during rehearsals, but during a quick break I broke all the rules and asked John why he'd switched me to soprano 2. "Have I lost my high notes? You can tell me." But it wasn't that. He was simply low on second sopranos. "If you can find a first soprano to take your place," he said, "you can switch." Right. Very clever of him. Like there was a first soprano anywhere in the world who would ever step down voluntarily. So that was that. I was a soprano 2. No take-backs. No rescue.

Rehearsal resumed. Now I not only had to learn this impossibly difficult piece, I had to sing it as a soprano 2. That was going to be my payback for all the hard work I knew was in front of me. I looked down. *So*, I thought without pleasure, *what nonsensical unpretty note am I expected to find and sing next?* I resented all the soprano 1s around me. The best notes secured for themselves, they were completely oblivious to my misery. They barely paid attention to what the rest of the choir had to do. I knew because I used to be one of them. As far as they were concerned the rest of us sang some insignificant notes that they passed by on their way to the beautiful, soaring top. Why did all the other people in the choir even bother coming? "Are you even aware that the altos are singing?" John once asked the sopranos. *No. Not really.* When John gave the signal to begin, I picked up my music in defeat.

WHY DOES IT seem like bad things always happen in clusters? That night I was in a bad mood before I'd even read about my new part assignment. Minutes before leaving for choir an e-mail had popped up from the man I thought I was going to marry but who had dumped me instead. Although it had been over between us for a few years, for just a millisecond my heart swelled with hope that somewhere in that e-mail he'd give me a good enough reason to forgive him, beg me to take him back, and make my long-imagined dream come true. I may not be religious, but I still hold on to miracles. Earlier in the year, when Chesley Sullenberger successfully landed a disabled plane in the Hudson River, I ran over and followed the plane the whole way as it floated down the water. It was such a wonderful, impossible happy ending and it actually happened. I didn't want to let go. I stayed beside the river and that plane long into the night, and many hours after I could actually see it.

Apparently some small part of me hadn't let go of this guy either. Perhaps because shortly after meeting him he was sitting in the audience at the Choral Society's spring concert, when the choir sang Mozart's *Great Mass in C Minor*. We began to fall in love to music that is in some ways one of the greatest love notes ever written. Mozart expressly wrote the exquisitely tender soprano solos for his new bride, Constanze. When she sang them at the premiere, she became more than just the recipient of a searingly beautiful expression of love, but also the most fortunate instrument of its conveyance. Mozart would have understood Constanze's voice intimately, her full range of highs and lows, the tones, the colors; and he used his genius to beautifully and expertly inhabit her, sending her voice out into the world to ripple through other human hearts as it had through his, to dance, twirl, bask, and play—the full truth of his passion both out there for all the world to see and hear and also reverberating inside her, in a deeply personal way.

When I looked out and sang to the crowd of close to a thousand, I borrowed Mozart's brilliance and focused the truth of that music on the heart of only one. Afterward, we stood together on Broadway, fumbling for words but smiling, smiling, smiling, the headlights of car after car flashing behind us like cameras on a red carpet. The intermittent blare of their horns felt like bursts of uncontainable affirmation. Soon after that night, we began to plan our future. Every heartbreak I had ever endured was worth it because it led to him, I thought. Then he dumped me. Without explanation.

I was so stunned I spent the next few weeks holed up on my couch, just wallowing and watching television. One night a TV movie about alien abduction came on. The main character, a little girl, said: "We're all standing on the edge of a cliff. All the time, every day. A cliff we're all going over. Our choice isn't about that. Our choice is about whether we want to go kicking and screaming or whether we might want to open our eyes and our hearts to what happens once we start to fall."

I wasn't exactly kicking and screaming. I'd gone over that cliff in a tight little ball with my eyes closed, hoping it wouldn't hurt too much when I reached the end of my descent. It never occurred to me that maybe falling wasn't what I thought it was going to be, that perhaps there was something in between death and miracles and I should open my eyes, spread my arms wide, and see. Three words immediately came to me: *Embrace the fall.*

My relationship with this man was over and there was nothing I could do about it. Okay, embrace the fall. And I tried. Really hard. But this guy continued to torture me by returning to my life, then exiting again and again; happy endings held out and then yanked away, each time also without explanation. Fortunately, I finally pulled myself together and said Enough. Don't call me, don't e-mail me, don't send me instant messages. I never want to hear from you again.

And now here he was, back again, e-mailing me about what

turned out to be a mundane, nonpersonal business matter. Still, I was determined not to let a momentary disappointment, however intense, ruin the one thing I could count on in life. I deleted his e-mail, pulled out a new top I'd just bought, put my hair up, and headed crosstown to choir practice.

A half hour later I was downgraded to soprano 2, unable to find my notes, too devastated to even cry. The brave front I'd put on along with my new blouse was shattered, and before I could stop it a list of every reason to despair rushed through my head: my heart still flutters for someone who clearly hasn't thought of me in "that way" in years, I was old, no one would ever love me, and now I was no longer even a soprano 1. The one thing I supposedly could count on had been taken away, like that.

Then, only a minute later, my mood and my world changed. I hit my first correct soprano 2 note. I don't even know where it came from, but I got it right. It was a D. The soprano 1 to my right was singing the B flat above me. I love that glorious high B flat and I should have been apoplectic with envy about not getting to sing it myself, but instead I was pinned to that D, vibrating with a wondrous musical rapport I'd never felt before. I was feeling harmony. Not just singing it, but physically feeling it. It was a rush. You don't experience this when you're singing the melody. I was completely in the power of the sound we were making together and I just stood there, afraid to move, thinking, *Don't end, don't end, don't end.* And it took nothing. Nothing. A couple of notes. A D against a

B flat. That's it. Two notes and I went from a state of complete misery and lonesomeness to such an astonishing sense of communion it was like I'd never sung with the choir before.

It was similar to falling in love for the first time. When it happens you think, "Oh my god I have never felt this rapturously together with another person before. This is what it's all about. This is what living is for." Except I was feeling this with a whole roomful of people. And I could return to the euphoria week after week after week. With just a couple of notes.

I tried to catch the eye of everyone around me who wasn't a soprano 1. *I get it.* First sopranos don't feel this. You hear it, but you don't *feel* it. You don't know that those lowly peasants making a nice vocal cushion for you to step on had parts that were every bit as rapturous as yours.

I had experienced something approaching this whenever I'd sung next to an alto, tenor or bass. There's also the almost erotic thrill I get sometimes when I'm next to the men's section and they're singing something with power and gusto, like the Confutatis maledictis section from Mozart's *Requiem*. But I'd never had this intense visceral sensation of literally resonating in harmony with the people around me. What was happening? If it was real it could be studied and measured. I started looking for science books with *music* in the title.

While searching through Daniel J. Levitin's book *This is Your Brain on Music,* I found a fascinating section about a related issue: overtones. This is when we sing and the church sings with us. It's an acoustical phenomenon. We sing and we

can hear notes that didn't come from us, resonating high up in
the rafters. It's as if we've excited the Heavens, who now can't
resist joining us. But it's not just any notes. They're always at
an interval that produces a nice harmony. John sometimes has
the sopranos drop out to demonstrate this. We stop singing,
but our notes magically continue, floating somewhere above
our heads, quietly, in this strange ethereal tone. Churchgoers
may once have thought there were angels up there.

Levitin's book explains what's really happening. When
a note is sung (or played), it vibrates at a certain frequency
called the fundamental. But it also simultaneously vibrates at
other frequencies in a mathematically elegant and harmonic
way. Those are the overtones (also referred to as harmonics
or the harmonic series). This is what gives notes and instruments their tone and color. The structure of the Grace Church
sanctuary simply makes them easier to hear. It's like the physical world wants and must have harmony. When we sing in
harmony the universe presents us with a feeling so fantastic it
guarantees that we'll do it again and again. When we don't,
the universe steps up and provides the harmony for us.

The choral conductor Robert Shaw writes that "the basic
premise of music-making is unity—and unanimity—and,
in its nonliturgical sense, communion." Perhaps the pleasure
of harmony, and communion, is an evolutionary reward for
cooperation. Harmony is about relationships, after all: the relationship of the notes to each other, our voices to each other,
and to the overtones rippling out with every sound we make.

I looked into the history of *The Chichester Psalms*—which I now loved—to see if I could discover anything about Bernstein's ideas about harmony. He made these feelings I was experiencing happen, after all. In August 1964 Bernstein was commissioned to write something for the Southern Cathedrals Festival taking place in England the following summer. Apparently he wasn't the least bit anxious about finishing in time, because he didn't even get started until the spring. It barely caused an interruption in his fabulous life. Working out of his fifteen-room duplex on Park Avenue, and in between "visits to the ballet with Mrs. Jacqueline Kennedy," he tossed off the entire piece in a little over two months. It took me longer to learn my one small part. He was so last minute about it that the orchestra's first rehearsal was on the day of the concert. "All we can do now is pray," Bernstein said about the upcoming performance. He later wrote that "the orchestra was swimming in the open sea. They simply didn't know it." How could they? But everything turned out all right. According to Bernstein, "the glorious acoustics of Chichester Cathedral cushion everything so that even mistakes sound pretty." Two weeks later Bernstein was back to his glamorous whirlwind of a life, at the *Ed Sullivan Show,* listening to the Beatles rehearse for their upcoming appearance.

The reason Bernstein was able to write the *Psalms* so quickly was due in part to the fact that he cheated. "I think many of us would be very delighted if there was a hint of *West Side Story* about the music," the Dean of Chichester wrote, encouraging him. Bernstein was all over that one. *West Side Story* was eight years old by this time, but Bernstein had a snippet that was cut from the prologue that he was dying to use somewhere. He put it in the second movement of the *Psalms,* in a section where the women drop out and the men fiercely sing, *"Lamah rag'shu goyim / Ul'umim yeh'gu rik?"* That's Hebrew and it translates to "Why do the nations rage, / And the people imagine a vain thing?" (From the second Psalm of the Bible.) The first time we sang it John said, "You can hear the Jets and the Sharks." And it does sound like two gangs running and shouting through the city streets. It's violent, but it's also exuberant. There must be something invigorating about a battle, about going wild like that. (Originally, the two opposing groups in *West Side Story* were going to be Jews and Catholics instead of Americans and Puerto Ricans. If Bernstein had written it today it would be about Muslims and Christians.)

Right after the men conclude their West Side Story storming-through-the-streets, Bernstein's direction for the sopranos is to sing as if we were "blissfully unaware of threat." Composers write all sorts of directions for the choir (and orchestra). These directions are called dynamics and expression markings, and they provide instructions for volume, style, and mood. Often the commands are simple, such as how loud or soft to sing. Sometimes they are more poetic, like *en mourant,* or "dying down," which calls for a simultaneous decrease in both volume and tempo. Bernstein was on the poetic side. For instance, instead of a simple *p* for *piano* (meaning "softly and quietly") he wrote *dolce, tranquillo,* or "tenderly." So what threat are we supposed to be blissfully unaware of? At that point in the music we're singing dueling Psalms with the men. While the women sing a relatively peaceful section from the Twenty-third Psalm—"Thou preparest a table before me in the presence of my enemies, / Thou anointest my head with oil, / My cup runneth over"—the men quietly resume Psalm 2, a more subdued but still present mob.

I found lots of death and raging in the *Psalms,* but nothing specifically about the bliss of harmony. Until I noticed this connection. Bernstein begins the piece with the beginning of Psalm 100:

> Make a joyful noise unto the
> Lord all ye lands.
> Serve the Lord with gladness.
> Come before His presence with singing.

And then he ends with these words from Psalm 133:

> Behold how good,
> And how pleasant it is,
> For brethren to dwell
> Together in unity.

After all the raging and with the constant threat of death, in the end there's this. Singing and unity. We come together, in harmony. We know it was important to Bernstein by the dynamics he left for those final words. Before we start singing

"Behold how good, / And how pleasant it is," he wrote *lento possibile*. "As slow as possible." He wanted us to linger on what we were singing for as long as we could. He also used another device to make sure everyone paid attention. He marked the very last line with *pppp*. For "very, very, very, very softly and quietly." Extreme *piano*. A large group of people singing that faintly is more dramatic than shouting. The intensity is palpable. If you were falling asleep during a performance, it would wake you right up. The yearning of over one hundred very quiet voices reaches out with a command to listen that is impossible to ignore. And in the *Psalms* the message was this: the world, the universe, and Leonard Bernstein, want harmony. It's all we have to hold on to. Behold how good it is.

And how long it has been around. I recently learned that shortly after the universe was born it began to sing. Space was not silent then, as it is now. As pressure waves moved through the primordial gases of creation, it had an atmosphere (of sorts) that enabled sound. Using maps of the Cosmic Microwave Background radiation and computer programs that can map the path of those waves, astronomy professor Dr. Mark Whittle was able to analyze the historical record of that early expansion, and what he found was a sequence of notes. He also found that, like any note that rings out today, those notes had these key characteristics: a fundamental frequency and harmonics, or overtones. Even at the very beginning of time there were overtones.

When Whittle converted the first 400,000 years of the cosmic chorus into notes from a standard octave of an even-tempered scale (what we're used to hearing) and raised the pitch fifty octaves (to put it in range of the human ear), it gave the song a spooky *Carnival of Souls* feel. It's just eerie. Strange. It's what the dead would sound like if they could sing and were not particularly upset about being dead and were instead curiously exploring the other side. The notes were spread out in pitch, which is different from how we sing, so it doesn't make a particularly pretty song. It's more noisy. Still, it begins with a beautiful fall, a downward glissando of what sounds like airplanes diving. This settles into a low, almost muffled roar or booming, and ends with a higher-pitched hiss, which crescendos. (The universe gave the sopranos the last word.)

Whittle noticed something else. Over time, as the song died out, the chord evolved from a major third into a minor third. In a study of pitch patterns in human speech, Meagan Curtis of Tufts University's Music Cognition Lab found that when the participants in her study wanted to indicate sadness they used the minor third. This is a common device in music composition as well. It's interesting that when we want to express sorrow we use the exact same interval the universe did when the celestial song was ending. But there is no reason to mourn the close of that song. Those final tones brought us the stars and galaxies, Whittle says. The high-pitched hiss is the sound of the creation of the first generation of stars, "while the deep bass notes slowly dissolve to become the tapestry of galaxies which now fills all of space," left out there like a great cosmic symphonic score, charting the birth of everything.

In 1973, decades before Whittle made his startling observations, Leonard Bernstein said, "I believe that from the Earth emerges a musical poetry which is by the nature of its sources tonal. I believe that these sources cause to exist a phonology of music, which evolves from the universal known as the harmonic series." Pythagoras also thought the cosmos was harmonious. He had a theory called *musica universalis,* or "music of the spheres." Out there in the Heavens, Pythagoras believed, the movement of the planets made a harmonic sound. While the harmonics of the cosmic expansion are a little different from the harmonic series (and the mathematical relationship more complicated), I think Bernstein and Pythagoras would have loved learning that when the expanding universe filled spaces that it had never filled before, it filled them with song; that in a sense, everything—matter, the Earth, and us—came from the first and last song the universe ever sang, and the universe sang in harmony.

THE DAY AFTER my demotion to soprano 2, when I no longer needed comforting, John e-mailed me that composers do not view soprano 1 and 2 as "distinctly different voices." He explained that all sopranos are expected to be able to sing from the B-flat below middle C to a high B-flat. "So I tend to move people around for reasons of balance," he said, "that's all it is—it's never a judgment on an individual singer's lack of high notes. Soprano 2 is often more difficult musically and for that reason a lot of sopranos don't like to trouble with it and take the position that they don't like to sing 'that low' even when it's roughly equal in range or higher." Equal in range or higher? So I was going to get this joy *and* sing the high notes?

The following season I was singing next to my friend Barbara, who is a soprano 1. We were both singing the C above middle C, a favorite soprano 1 note, but my part required me to leave that C and step down one note, hold it for a beat, and then step down another and hold that for a beat. The briefest little dance and yet it made the prettiest sound so far in the piece. Barbara looked at me. "Was that the soprano 2 part?" she asked, astonished. I nodded. Behold how good it is. "I'm singing that next time," she said. I put an asterisk in the spot.

Not long after, my ex-boyfriend started e-mailing me yet again. I didn't respond and he kept sending e-mail. One day he just showed up at my apartment. I didn't go downstairs, and I didn't buzz him in. I practically punched the intercom button as I held it down and told him to once and for all leave me alone.

I remembered what happened the last time I buzzed him in after we'd broken up. It was just days after I'd sung at the wedding of Mike Young and Kim Ahearn, two choir members who'd met through the Choral Society the same year I'd met him. The wedding took place at Grace Church, of course. Kim had walked down the aisle past sprays of sunflowers, in a simple, backless, satin gown, while Mike stood at the altar in a fashionable, almost mod, black suit. They looked so stylish and handsome it could have been a photo shoot for *Vogue*. The church practically glowed with a sense of celebration. Kim was calm, Mike looked like he was ready to cry at any moment, and the rector, who'd been in his post for only eight days, was somewhere in-between. Each, in their own way, looked radiantly happy.

Everything about that day was light and bright, alive with love and music. They'd met through singing, and the first gift Mike ever gave Kim was a small wooden music box. It was at Christmas. After listening to every music box in the store, he chose the one that played "Jesu, Joy of Man's Desiring," the chorale used in Bach's cantata *Herz und Mund und Tat und Leben* (*Heart and Mouth and Deed and Life*). Two years later, they were sitting on a bench at Battery Park, looking out over New York Harbor and the Statue of Liberty. Mike presented Kim with the same music box, but this time with an engagement ring inside. When Kim walked down the aisle, "Jesu, Joy of Man's Desiring" was ringing throughout the church.

I should have been sad, singing at Mike and Kim's wedding. They'd met the same year my ex and I had met, and here they were, reveling to the strains of a joyous Bach cantata, and there I was, single. Again. But between the music and Mike and Kim's waves of joy, I found it impossible to not get carried away and cheerfully ride along. When I sang, all I cared about was not messing up on such an important day.

A few days after Mike and Kim's wedding, my ex was at the door with flowers and emphatic pleas to take him back—again. Then we went to breakfast, the movies, for a walk along the Hudson River, to my grandparents' old house in Queens, then finally to his house, where he fixed me dinner and told me he loved me, and that he was now in therapy. The day couldn't have been more awash with demonstrations of love, and I floated for hours like a bride walking down the aisle, the exuberant Sanctus movement from Mozart's *Mass in C Minor* pealing jubilantly around me from all sides.

We lasted a week. When I spoke to him on the phone for the last time the outpouring of love clamped abruptly shut and it was like inhaling dust.

That was when I retired to my couch and a TV movie about aliens made me realize I was living in a world of cartoon physics, hanging in midair like a doomed Wile E. Coyote, merely postponing the inevitable plunge. Embrace the fall. So I finally opened my eyes and my heart and took the fall, but not his calls, and I never buzzed him in again. What I hadn't realized, however, was there's always another cliff. This guy *still* periodically tries to contact me, sending e-mails I continue to ignore, or messages through mutual friends, which I never return. I might be momentarily thrown, but now, whenever life sends me over the cliff, I'm not kicking and screaming. I'm singing. Soprano 2.

Recitative
The Rubenstein Club

H enry Edward Krehbiel, an influential nineteenth-century music critic for the *New York Tribune,* once wrote, "A female chorus cannot be a success, and if you should form one of angels from heaven, with Saint Cecilia as conductress, I would say the same." Choral societies were spreading all over America, but for many of them women were welcome only when needed as soloists on the night of the performance. As far as Krehbiel was concerned, the appearance of New York's first all-female choral society was not only pointless, it was robbing men of the limited available financial support. It was "a pity," he wrote, "that so much energy and money should be expended when the results can only be of the most superficial interest."

In 1886 a group of young women had gone to see their former music teacher, William Rogers Chapman, conduct the all-male choral society that he'd recently formed. After the concert the girls surrounded him and begged him to let them continue to sing with him as well. Chapman agreed, and after rehearsing the women for several months, he scheduled a concert at the Society of Ethical Culture and invited some of the leading lights of New York's musical world to attend. Annie Louise Cary Raymond, a retired but still popular opera singer, was in the audience. "Make this a women's singing club," she said to Chapman afterward, "and I will sing with you." Chapman christened the fledgling group the Rubinstein Club, after his favorite composer, Anton Rubinstein, and soon other prominent female singers were clamoring to join.

For their first concert as the Rubinstein Club, sixty women sang from a program that included three selections by Anton Rubinstein and a Beethoven string quartet. It was a glittering affair. "When the concert was concluded," Krehbiel wrote in his first review of them, "Fifth Avenue and the side streets leading from it were crowded with carriages, which were as difficult to find as after a court ball." Then he cruelly added that the whole thing would have been a lot better if only men had been involved. "What a concert could be given if the Rubinstein and [all-male] Mendelssohn clubs were to co-operate. It would be worth ten years of sentimental trios and quartets for female voices floating about in the musical ether with no foundation to rest on. . . ." It was actually a relatively restrained review for Krehbiel, but it was the last time he would hold back. "A female chorus?" he wrote in a later piece. "You might as well expect a physician to discuss the value of treacle as an article of exclusive diet."

A few years and many critical pieces later, including one in which he wrote how "an evening of music written in two or three parts for women's voices exclusively is of necessity wearisome," Krehbiel dashed off yet another for *Harper's Weekly*. It was full of vitriol. He attacked the women's clothes, the flowers on the stage, and the fact that their concerts were by invitation only. Only the year before, Krehbiel had praised invitation-only concerts using the very established, all-male Mendelssohn Glee Club as an example. Evidently, invitation-only concerts, frivolous when women were performing, were virtuous when men were involved. Krehbiel even insulted the Rubinstein Club's audience for being there.

Chapman had had enough. He wrote to Krehbiel expressing his regret that Krehbiel believed his women's choral society was more social than musical and that the concerts were "notable more for the beautiful surroundings and the subscription list of society people than for the musical ability of the singers." Chapman concluded his letter by diplomatically asking for suggestions as to how they might improve.

His diplomacy went unrewarded. "I don't depreciate social influence," Krehbiel responded, "but when that is had in great measure there is a corresponding obligation to art." And on this point, he didn't see any hope for the Rubinstein Club. "I cannot be convinced that a female chorus has any reason to exist except it amuses itself and those who are willing to pay for it; surely it has no claim on artistic consideration, and could not have if it consisted wholly of Pattis." (He's referring to Adelina Patti, one of the biggest female opera stars of the day.)

If women's voices were not capable of great beauty, Chapman argued, why had composers like Schubert, Rubinstein, Rheinberger, and so many others "wasted so many hours on works for women's voices only?" Indeed. Within three months of hearing a group of women sing, Johannes Brahms had not only put together a women's singing society, he was composing for them. "The girls are so nice, fresh and enthusiastic, without being soft and sentimental," Brahms wrote. On some nights, even though they'd rehearsed until very late, no one, including Brahms, wanted the evening to end. After rehearsals his girls would "walk quite calmly into a garden and wake the people up at midnight with their singing." Antonio Vivaldi was even more progressive, writing for girls at the beginning of the eighteenth century. His "Gloria in D," which is sung all over the world every Christmas, is believed to have been written for a group of orphaned Venetian girls, who sang what is now the bass line up an octave.

"From your own statement," Chapman continued, "I must judge you a prejudiced party against women's voices in choirs: therefore, can you be a fair critic?" That said, the *Tribune* critic was expressing an opinion held by many at the time. Musical tastes then favored what was heard as the purer, sweeter tones of boys over girls. Krehbiel, a longtime supporter of choral societies, was, in fact, also in favor of choral societies with mixed voices. He described the uproar in response to the Handel and Haydn Society's admission of six women in 1815 as quaint. It was women's voices by themselves that bored him.

This point of view has not entirely gone away. Few women's choruses can fill halls the way all-male groups can. When I first joined the Choral Society of Grace Church, the Church had a boys' choir but not a girls'. At the time, I was told that girls' voices didn't sound beautiful until they matured and, repeating the view held in the nineteenth century, that boys' voices had a certain sweetness and a beautiful tone that girls' voices lacked. The response doesn't even make musical sense. All instruments (and the voice is an instrument) have different qualities of sound. One voice or instrument may, in fact, be sweeter, but what composer wants only sweet? Just as it's fair to say that a concert consisting of one instrument can get monotonous, it's equally true of a single-sex choir. Krehbiel's attitude and that of others like him is more a reflection of musical and political tastes than of any quality inherent in women's voices. Thankfully, Grace Church has progressed. In 1994, on the centennial of the boys' choir, the church established its first girls' choir.

Sadly, the Rubinstein Club doesn't appear to have lasted much beyond William Rogers Chapman's death in 1935 at age seventy-nine. His wife, Emma, took over for a while, but the last concert listing I could find for the group was in 1941. Perhaps, in the end, the club was more social than musical. The very polite reviews I came across may suggest that the Rubinstein Club was wanting artistically, even for those who didn't share Krehbiel's views about female singers. Chapman's musical selections for their concerts weren't helping, according to Krehbiel. Their programs were filled with what Krehbiel described as "sugary nothings," and part-songs and glees that belonged "to the domain of what might be called weak chamber music." Even Chapman's friends agreed his choices were sometimes overly sentimental. (I have to wonder what Krehbiel would have made of contemporary pieces such as Ysaye M. Barnell's "Soundbite from Beijing" or Bernice Johnson Reagon's "Ella's Song." Written by women for women, they are anything but sugary and weak.) Further, the element of high society that had so rankled Krehbiel was in evidence in the membership, some of whom came from the highest society of all, Mrs. Astor's Four Hundred (said to be the number of people who could fit into Mrs. Astor's ballroom and the most fashionable and exclusive list in New York at the time). It was also evident in the place they chose to sing. After trying out various venues around the city, the Rubinstein Club settled into what was then the new grand ballroom at the Waldorf-Astoria Hotel (owned by the Astors). When the original structures were torn down in 1929 to make room for the Empire State Building, they followed the hotel to its new location at Fiftieth Street and Park Avenue.

But if membership in high society is a worthy point of criticism, the lists of associate members of the all-male Mendelssohn Glee Club (the people who supported them financially) is a veritable who's who of New York's upper crust, including Margaret Astor herself and her husband, William Backhouse Astor, Theodore Roosevelt and his daughter Alice, J. P. Morgan, Louis Comfort Tiffany, and many others. When the *Titanic* sank on April 15, 1912, Frederic K. Seward, a Glee Club member who'd been on board, still managed to make it to rehearsal a week later to tell them "all about his experience in the horrible *Titanic* disaster." And, like the coal miners who sang after the Wilkes-Barre disaster, less than two weeks after the luxury liner went down, the Mendelssohn Glee Club went ahead with a concert at the Hotel Astor, even though the Astors' son John Jacob Astor IV was among those who had perished.

In the end, without a recording there is no way of knowing how well the women sang. It could be that the club owes its demise to the simple fact that if the world isn't quite ready for all-female choirs now, it certainly wasn't ready back then. While the Mendelssohn Glee Club, founded in 1866, continues today, few if any remember the Rubinstein Club, and although they performed there every year for over forty years, the Waldorf-Astoria no longer has any record of them in its archives.

Messiah

Written by George Frideric Handel in 1741

Performed by the Choral Society of Grace Church
in the Winter, 1982

I joined the Choral Society of Grace Church when I was twenty-six years old. My brief marriage had just ended, and after a series of relationships that didn't last long enough to legitimately be called relationships, I found myself in church, only I wasn't looking for God. I'd spent the previous few nights sitting on the floor in the middle of my living room, rocking back and forth and crying about yet another painful breakup. What can I say, I was young. Everything felt like the end of the world then. (I wasn't much better more than twenty years later, but I did learn one thing: if you're going to curl up into a ball of misery, the couch is more comfortable than the floor.) Night after night I sat there in the dark, listening to cab doors opening and closing underneath my window, and the sounds of people getting in and out, all talking and laughing on their way to and from parties, restaurants, and dates.

I'd been dreaming of living in New York City ever since I was nine years old. *Sex and the City* wouldn't air for decades, so my New York City–girl role model was Marlo Thomas in *That Girl*. The city-girl-life highlights in both shows, however, were surprisingly similar. I'd have my own apartment, a fulfilling career, a fabulous wardrobe, a wide array of accomplished friends, and dates at the ballet, gallery openings, or some slightly dangerous club downtown. Nowhere in my fantasy was there a job hooking computers up to each other by day, or going out with guys I'd never hear from again—and didn't want to—at night (*Sex and the City* could have helped me there, or *Girls*). More than anything else, I wanted to figure out what I was doing wrong, stop it, then get myself off the floor and back into a party dress.

After a few nights of trying unsuccessfully to fantasize a better version of what I saw as my stalled and flailing life, I knew I had to get off that floor. I went over to my desk, pulled out a pen and piece of paper, and made a list. I've always been big on lists. I wrote down all the things that made me happy, sticking to items that were easily attainable:

- The blue-orange light that happens around 7 to 8 p.m. (aka dusk)
- The pools of water left after the tide recedes that have fish in them (tide pools; I must not have known they have a name)

- Staple Street (a small, back-in-time street in downtown Manhattan)
- Van Gogh's almond trees and irises (clearly I'd just been to the Met)
- Air shafts (so New York, and so romantically dreary)

And then I wrote something unexpected:

- Singing

And with that word, like some sort of musical near-death experience, my entire singing life flashed before my eyes. Singing at family functions, and my normally critical mother smiling and encouraging me; jumping on a table when I was a teenager to sing the Partridge Family song "I Think I Love You" in order to convince my friends that this was a great song; singing along with the radio at the top of my lungs when I was driving; singing and dancing around my apartment before I left for work or a party; singing made-up tribute songs to my pets ("Who is the greatest cat in the whole wide world, tra-la-la-la"); singing show tunes on the street after seeing a particularly fabulous Broadway musical. Later, singing along at concerts, at parties, at basically every opportunity. Singing had punctuated all the best moments of my life. And created them.

One memory stood out from all the others. My high school boyfriend had just told me he was going to be singing with a church choir that Christmas. I wanted to join him, but I hadn't been to church since I was twelve years old. The briefest battle in the history of the world inside my head immediately commenced: be true to my agnosticism or sing Christmas carols? On the night of the concert I wore hiking boots under my choir robes to signal my protest of organized religion, walked down the aisle, and began what would become my lifelong history of being so happy singing I'd have to fight tears. Someone had turned the inside of that church into a holiday wonderland, and there were pots of poinsettias and lilies in every available corner and candles of all sizes twinkling throughout like the lights on Christmas trees. Everywhere I looked, from the priest vestments to the altar and the jewelry adorning the parishioners, was alight with shimmering gold. By the time we got to "O Holy Night" I was practically hyperventilating with joy.

That's it, I thought all those years ago, sitting there in my Manhattan walk-up. Christmas carols. Singing. This was a sure-fire way to stop my suffering. It was August when I had this revelation, and I knew that churches all over Manhattan would soon start holding rehearsals for their holiday concerts. If I hurried, I could find a choir somewhere and become a member. I picked myself up off the floor and started looking. In a lifetime of spectacularly bad moves, it would turn out to be the best one I've ever made.

THE TRICK WAS to find just the right church. I had only two criteria. It had to be beautiful, of course, the loveliest church in Manhattan if possible (I can be very competitive).

And, because I would be heading there every week for rehearsals, it had to be easy to get to. I soon discovered that there
are a lot of churches in Manhattan, twenty or thirty within
walking distance of my West Village apartment alone. I set
out wearing sensible heels and carrying a map with the closest
churches marked with X's, but in the end it was all unneces-
sary. I was a few churches into my quest when I walked inside
Grace Church at Tenth and Broadway, and I knew this was
it. My musical home.

Grace Church was designed in 1843 by James Renwick
Jr., the same James Renwick who designed the more famous
St. Patrick's Cathedral uptown. I learned much later that he
won the commission to design Grace Church when he was
only twenty-four years old. I couldn't help comparing. James
Renwick Jr. at twenty-six: standing proudly on Broadway,
surveying the work on what would become one of the most
beautiful buildings in the world. Me at twenty-six: going out
with all the wrong guys and barely able to get up off the floor.

I walked down the aisle of Grace Church very slowly that
first day. I stepped out of time, captured by the same elements
I'm drawn to today. First, the memorials. Not the glorious
stained-glass windows or the statues of saints and martyrs.
I wanted to read every plaque commemorating the Grace
Church dead. Like Edith Corse Evans, "Who In The Midst
Of Life Gave Herself For Others On The Titanic." Edith was
one of only four first-class female passengers on the ship to
die. As far as I could tell she died because she was single.

She was only thirty-six, but she gave up her seat to another woman because, as she was reported to have said, "You have children waiting at home." I thought about that for a moment. What would I have done? I looked into Edith's story later. It turns out she had given her seat to a woman who was fifty-eight years old at the time and whose children were all grown. When Edith helped the older woman into the lifeboat at 2:05 a.m., she didn't know she was giving up her life. A seaman had called out to her that another boat was about to be put down. But there were only two lifeboats left by this time, both had problems, and Edith didn't make it onto either of them. "Love Is Strong As Death," her memorial plaque reads. *Right. I'm never getting on a boat again.*

After reading all the memorials I could make out, I took in the windows, the pews, the figures carved into the stone, the vaulted ceiling above me, and the tiles below my feet. The altar at the end of the church was so brilliantly white it stood out from the gray stone around it and seemed to vibrate and hover. Although there was a lot about Grace Church that was properly solemn and dark, overall the feel was light. I could imagine funerals being held here, but I could more easily imagine weddings and baptisms, and more important, holiday concerts. This was the place.

So I did what any distraught woman in search of a choir would do: I fled. I was afraid to approach anyone in person. Priests make me anxious. I don't understand their total commitment to something that to me seems so unreal. I called when I got home. Good news and bad news. I was welcome to join, I was told, but first I would have to audition. *Wait, what?*

I didn't have to audition for that other church choir I sang with as a teenager. The one and only time I ever auditioned for anything was for a part in *Bye Bye Birdie* in high school. I showed up for the audition, stood at the piano, and panicked. My voice immediately went flat. I looked at the director. Did he notice? Of course he did. I looked at everyone else in the room. Did they notice? Of course they did, but they saw how mortified I was and very kindly looked away. I tried to get my voice back up to the right pitch, but my throat was locked on the wrong note and soon I was fighting tears. I wanted to stop and say, "No, wait! I know I sucked just now, but I can actually sing. Give me a chance." I knew my voice wasn't particularly beautiful, but I could sing in tune (except at auditions, I was learning horribly) and I was just hoping for a part in the background somewhere. But at sixteen years old I didn't have either the poise or the nerve to speak up for myself and instead I left the room in shame. Needless to say, I didn't get a part of any kind. This must have hurt me more than I realized, because it's a moment I still relive. Forty years later I still want those people to know I can at least sing in tune.

When I discovered that I would have to audition for the choir at Grace Church, I contemplated dropping the plan right there. I didn't want to fail again. What if I went flat again? But I didn't want to go back to sobbing on the floor.

I looked at my list once more. Nope. Nothing useful there besides singing. I scheduled an audition.

THE PERSON CONDUCTING my audition was Frank Cedric Smith, the Grace Church organist and music director at the time. He, with his wife Dilys, cofounded the Choral Society of Grace Church in 1974, although initially it was called the Grace Church Community Chorus. It was quite a triumph for Smith. Grace Church has a history of being very particular about its musical program, and battles of one kind or another have been fought for 128 years to prevent me or anyone like me from ever climbing the steps to the chancel, the space in front of the altar where the choir sings. By "anyone like me" I mean nonprofessional singers.

When Grace Church was built, singing was left to a quartet of opera stars and a small professional chorus who sang in the galley above the front door. Even the congregation were encouraged to keep their mouths shut. Once, during sexton Isaac H. Brown's reign (1845–1880), a visitor to the church started innocently singing along with a hymn. Brown ran down the aisle to stop him, his swallow-tailed coat flapping. "We hire the choir to do the singing in this church!"

Grace Church was high society in those days. To be married in Grace Church, or buried following a service there, was the height of social achievement, and those achievements were regularly reported in the *New York Times*. No interlopers allowed. Herman Melville, who lived behind Grace Church until 1849, wrote a short story featuring the church in 1854. In it he describes the church as very fashionable, with a "noble string of flashing carriages" outside. When the protagonist tries to enter he's told they have no galleries and is turned away. "They didn't entertain poor folks," Melville wrote. The story was submitted to and rejected by *Putnam's Monthly* magazine because the church was so transparently Grace Church, and the "fat-paunched, beadle-faced man" was immediately recognizable as Isaac Brown.

But the church staff wasn't always snobbish. When P. T. Barnum's most famous performers, the little people Tom Thumb and Lavinia Warren, announced their engagement and their intention to be married in Grace Church, many balked, including P. T. Barnum, who had visions of larger tickets sales dancing in his head. Barnum wanted to hold the wedding at the Academy of Music, a popular music hall that could hold a greater number of paying customers. The Grace Church congregation called the couple mountebanks, but Rev. Thomas House Taylor was more compassionate. When one parishioner wrote Reverend Taylor calling Tom Thumb a monstrosity, Taylor shot back that Charles Stratton (Tom Thumb's real name) was "no more a monstrosity than you are." "It is true we are little," Stratton had written Reverend Taylor, "but we are as God made us . . . we are simply man and woman of like passions and infirmities, with you and other mortals. . . ." The wedding took place in the church on

February 10, 1863. A platform was built before the chancel so people could see the couple, and some of the most famous New Yorkers of the day, Mrs. Astor, Mrs. Cornelius Vanderbilt, and General Ambrose E. Burnside, were among those who filled the church to capacity, standing on the cushions in their pews in order to see even better.

A few decades later, a battle of another sort would take place inside the church. For much of the nineteenth century an expensive choir was what the stylish and wealthy congregants of Grace Church demanded. "They want to enjoy the five thousand dollar choir," one New Yorker wrote. And Grace Church delivered. It was famous for the quality of its music, and a typical music program consisted of Mozart and Beethoven and was described as "less ecclesiastical and more ornate." The great opera singers who regularly performed there also helped with the much needed task of filling the pews. When the celebrated operatic mezzosoprano Maria Malibran sang at Grace Church, attendance records were shattered. But by the end of the century Malibran was long gone and the music to which listeners were "compelled to listen Sunday after Sunday, year in and year out," one *New York Times* piece described, had devolved into a lot of chanting and antiquated Doric fugues and was "altogether too dry." At the same time, amateur singing was on the rise, and choral societies had started sprouting up to give people an opportunity to sing. This caused similar stirrings inside the church. In 1892 members of the church started floating the idea of instituting a vested choir of men and boys (essentially a choir in robes and surplices, a kind of tunic).

The congregation was divided. Vested choirs were an innovation and considered "popish" by some. But others saw it as a way out of their musical doldrums. After a seemingly endless debate of pros and cons, the church put it to a vote. The final tally was so close the church struck a compromise. The quartet of professional singers would continue to sing above the door in the gallery, and space would be added to the chancel for a new choir of men and boys. Having women in a vested church choir was one step too far at first. Professional opera singers aside, people were not interested in the voices of women in the nineteenth century; ladies could barely speak in public then, much less sing. When Verdi premiered his *Requiem* in a church in Milan in 1874, he had to negotiate with the archbishop for permission to allow women in the chorus. The archbishop finally agreed, but only if the women stood behind screens, dressed from head to toe in black, wearing Taliban-like mourning veils.

Over the next year, while the music library was expanded, the Grace Church Choir School was established to train the boys, and buildings went up to house them and their teachers. On Ascension Day the new choir triumphantly made its debut. "The music of Grace Church has been completely revolutionized," the Rector wrote in exhilaration. Soon after, the professional quartet was completely disbanded. (The new vested choir wasn't strictly an amateur choir, as everyone was paid, even the boys, although more modestly than the quartet. But they were more closely tied to the community of the church and felt less like hired hands.) A smaller choir of men, boys, and now women took the place of the quartet in the gallery. Two decades later one congregant was still grumbling about the presence of women. He wrote to the editor of the *New York Times* claiming that the women were bringing the choir down, that the "distractions of social life outweigh the importance of regular rehearsals in the minds of ladies." But by this time it was slowly becoming acceptable for women to study music, and as the joys of singing were awakened in them, too, and attitudes gradually changed, they successfully fought for their chance to raise their voices along with the men.

Music at Grace Church flourished. For a time. Then came the Depression. The boarding school for the boys had to be shut down. Finding and recruiting boys became increasingly difficult, and to make up for the deficiency, girls and women were *actively* recruited into the choir. Then World War II erupted. For the next twenty years the church struggled to keep up musically. By the time Frank Smith, an accomplished organist and choir conductor, was hired in 1960, the church had lost its musical luster and the newly formed music committee pinned all its hopes on Smith: bring back our days of musical glory.

The letter offering him the position contained two demands: resuscitate the boys' choir and get rid of the women.

"The women have sung well, very well, indeed, but, as long as they are in the chancel the boys will scarcely sing." The music committee did what had to be done to support Smith. They came up with money for choir scholarships and gave him a dual appointment as the master of music at Grace Church school. This provided Smith with the opportunity to spot and nurture the boys with the most vocal promise. In four years, Smith went from directing a group of six boys to a robust band of twenty-five.

Music at the church once again began to thrive. But Smith not only wanted to expand the congregation's opportunities for singing, he wanted to extend those opportunities to the community outside the church. His idea was welcomed because a community choir was seen as a form of outreach. Gone were the days when Grace Church had them lining up in the finest carriages in the nineteenth century and Rolls-Royces in the early twentieth. Church attendance had declined everywhere, and changes to some of the surrounding neighborhood had also had an effect. Union Square park, to the north, for example, had become a go-to destination for drug dealers and others with nothing left to lose, and over the years, fewer people were making their way to Grace Church. Smith believed music could bring them back. In 1974 a community chorus of amateur singers, both men and women, was established. You didn't have to be a member of Grace Church, or even an Episcopalian. In fact, you didn't have to practice any religion at all. A love and talent for singing were all that were required. For their first concert, a group of close to forty singers sang Handel's *Messiah,* and there was no charge, only a request for a donation.

When I showed up at the church almost a decade later for my audition, I was taken to the music room, the same room that had been added a century before to give the choir boys a place to practice. The open closets at the front of the room were filled with choir robes and piles and piles of well-used music scores. It was like the classrooms of my youth. Everything on the walls was hung at kid's-eye level, all the framed pictures of composers, scattered inspirational sayings, and children's drawings and gold-starred papers. It made me feel safe momentarily. I took a deep breath, looked Frank in the eye, and started babbling.

"I can't sing very well," I blurted out, saying what I had wanted to say all those years ago at my high school audition. "I mean I'm not awful or anything, but I know I'm not great either. Okay not great at all, but I sing in tune and I don't sing very loud, so even if I make a mistake I won't mess up anyone around me. But apparently in auditions I go flat, so if that happens could you please take my word for it that I can actually sing in tune? I'm not lying, I promise. Except, everybody probably says that, don't they? But, er, um, oh God. Oh, please please please just let me in the choir. I'm begging you."

Frank looked at me; was I finished? Then he smiled and said, "Well, let's hear what you sound like." I don't remember what I sang for him, but I didn't go flat. I was so relieved I wanted to scream. But there still was the matter of my not-so-great voice. I looked up at Frank. My happiness is in your hands, I thought. "It's true, you don't have a pretty voice," Frank told me bluntly. "But your pitch is solid. Okay, welcome to the Choral Society."

That was it. It was all over in seconds. I finally did scream a little. Maybe I even did a little dance. I would like to think I hugged Frank or kissed him, but I'm sure I was too shy. I knew from his expression, though, that he was aware of how happy he had made me. All these years later I can still see his face. He beamed down at me as if he knew he was giving me the best gift in the world. He looked like a man who knew he was somebody's hero.

A few months later I was singing Handel's *Messiah*. Written in 1741, it's an enormously popular choral work, and arguably the best-known. It tells the story of Jesus Christ, from his birth to his ascension into Heaven, and Handel wrote the music for the text in a blisteringly productive twenty-four days. As long as Frank was in charge of the choir, every Christmas we sang Handel's *Messiah*.

The *Messiah* score is hundreds of pages long, and each page is filled with endlessly cascading notes that initially were just a meaningless and terrifying blur. It gave me a panic attack. At first. But the people around me opened to the exact same pages and, astoundingly, began to sing. Luckily, I'd briefly taken piano lessons as a child, just long enough to learn to read music. I struggled, but after a while I got the hang of turning the notes into song. In one rehearsal my whole musical world changed. I'd never sung a masterpiece before. "When he chooses," Mozart wrote about Handel, "he strikes like a thunderbolt." I will always love the carols of my childhood, but this was Christmas music for grown-ups—for coal miners and anyone who have ever had to walk in darkness. The *Messiah* went straight past tinsel and twinkling lights and into the full range and truth of human experience. I haven't been able to get through the holidays without it since.

One year, long after Frank Smith retired in 1992, when the Choral Society stopped performing the *Messiah* annually, I got my *Messiah* fix by participating in the annual Handel's *Messiah* sing at Avery Fisher Hall at Lincoln Center. A "sing" is what choir people do for fun, and it's usually in the summer, when most choirs are on hiatus. Anyone who wants to can show up at various places around the city to sing the usual choral favorites, such as Mendelssohn's *Elijah* or the Bach *Mass in B Minor*. But the granddaddy of all sings is the Avery Fisher Hall *Messiah* sing, and that's in December. It's a monster. Over three thousand people show up. There are twenty-one choruses in the *Messiah*, and at the Avery Fisher Hall sing we do seventeen, with a different conductor for every chorus. (A chorus is what the choir sings, versus the solos.) It feels like a pep rally. Every time a new conductor takes the stage, everyone from his or her choir stands and shouts. We all want our own conductor to out-conduct the rest in this raucous, loud night of singing, cheering, and celebration. It's Christmas!

We're in New York City! At Avery Fisher Hall! Singing the "Hallelujah Chorus"! The collected sound of thousands of people may not be as precise or as quietly beguiling as the chamber chorus (a small group of singers) Handel intended, and there are always the people who can't sing as well as they think, but none of that matters. Even if you walked in darkness right up until the moment of arriving, by the end of the night you walk out and onto the streets of the city as high as a kite on endorphins and good will.

Toward the Unknown Region

Written by Ralph Vaughan Williams in 1906

**Performed by the Choral Society of Grace Church
in the Spring, 2007**

It was January and as usual I was heading east on Eleventh Street, to the first rehearsal for our yearly spring concert. I've become intimately acquainted with the changing seasons on Eleventh Street. For instance, there's a stretch where for a brief time during the spring the cherry blossoms are so abundant and so lush they make a big, fat, fluffy white-and-pink canopy that stretches from sidewalk to sidewalk. It's a dazzling display. The best part, however, is when the petals begin to fall. It makes me wish New York City were car free. I want to be able to walk down the center of the street like I'm in the middle of my own botanical ticker-tape parade. I'd raise my arms to the skies and twirl around in this confettilike explosion of renewal and possibility and pretend it's all for me. The spring is when choirs all over the city are singing lines like "deliver the souls of all the faithful departed from the pains of hell and from the bottomless pit." Or "I tremble and fear at the coming desolation and wrath. Day of wrath, calamity and misery, great and exceedingly bitter day." Choral singing was once exclusively a church thing, and it would appear that this is the message the religious want to give us at this lovely time of year: don't get too excited about those cherry blossoms that have already begun to perish, because they won't last forever and neither will you.

EVERYTHING I SING today began centuries ago with a bunch of monks chanting. At first they all sang the same thing, the same melody, which wasn't terribly melodic. The earliest chants, called plainsong chants, went up or down only a half a step or two, and there was never any harmony. Eventually they added a second voice or line, which was usually a fourth below. Over time more parts were added. Around the eleventh century the different parts starting becoming more independent, and each singer began to follow his own melodic line. As the pieces became more complicated it was no longer possible to simply memorize and repeat them, and a system of musical notation began to evolve. Something else started happening in the last centuries of the Middle Ages. The music, which was meant to glorify God, was now pretty glorious in and of itself, and the progressively more inventive pieces were becoming more and more of a pleasure to sing.

By the fifteenth century the music could no longer be contained within the monastery walls. It had spread to churches, chapels, and cathedrals, and pieces weren't being written for monks alone anymore, but for congregations. The composers, whose names were now being recorded along with the notes, continued to experiment with harmony, rhythm, and what voices could do, and by end of the Renaissance they were coming up with arrangements for up to eight different voice lines and sometimes many more. (This is when parts for soprano 2s start showing up.)

There are various names for each of the parts, depending on the year and the country, but here is an abbreviated summary of the voice-part history. The tenors were first. Their name comes from the latin word *tenere,* which means "to hold," and which more or less describes what those first monks were doing during a chant—they were holding the melody line. The ones who sang below came to be known as the basses (from *contratenor bassus,* "lower than the tenor") and the ones who sang above became the altos (from *contratenor altus,* "higher than the tenor"). The soprano line came last. I like how conductor John Maclay tells our choir the story: "An alien ship landed and out walked the sopranos." Their name comes from the latin word *sopra,* which means "from above," and the soprano part was originally sung by men or boys (as was the alto part) or castrati. That was due to the church's attitude toward women, so nicely summed up in St. Paul's dictum: *Mulieres in ecclesiis taceant.* "Let women keep silent in church." (Thanks a heap, St. Paul.) There are other in-between parts, such as the baritone, who comes between the tenor and the bass, but typically a choir consists of soprano-tenor-alto-bass, who are occasionally broken up into soprano 1s and 2s, alto 1s and 2s, and so on. "Four voice parts," John once said, "four personality disorders."

Even as early as the second century there were misgivings about where this was all headed. "I am inclined to approve of the custom of singing in church, in order that by indulging the ear weaker spirits may be inspired with feelings of devotion," St. Augustine wrote in his *Confessions*. "Yet when I find the singing itself more moving than the truth which it conveys, I confess that this is a grievous sin, and at those times I would prefer not to hear the singer." St. Augustine was concerned that singing would lead people away from God, while others were concerned that it would lead to the wrong God. In 1549 in Paris, a tailor was sentenced to be burned alive for owning the book of songs *Chansons spirituelles,* because of its anti-Catholic text. But over in England in 1605, when Catholics were being persecuted, a man was arrested for owning a copy of composer William Byrd's pro-Catholic *Gradualia.* Ultimately, though, it was impossible to repress or resist what was century by century becoming increasingly more beautiful.

Throughout the sixteenth and seventeenth centuries, choral music continued to blossom and flourish. This is when we start coming across composers whose pieces remain so eternally gorgeous and transcendent that they are still sung today, such as Giovanni Pierluigi da Palestrina and later Monteverdi, Schütz, and Purcell. (This is also because music printing wasn't common until the fifteenth century and few scores from previous centuries have survived.)

In the eighteenth century some Dublin charities invited George Frideric Handel to debut his *Messiah* in the new Musick Hall, which had just gone up in an area that was once the local fish market. While this wasn't the first time sacred music was performed outside a church, it was a sign of the times: sacred music had left the chancel and hit the stage. Concert halls were popping up everywhere, and composers had still more venues where they could spread their compositional wings. They weren't just church composers anymore. Handel's *Messiah* quickly became the ultimate crossover piece. Everyone wanted to sing it. Or hear it. Repeatedly.

At the same time, in America, parishioners were mangling hymns so badly that singing schools were established in order to teach people how to read music. Twentieth-century choral conductor Nym Cooke has a wonderful essay about this period in *The Cambridge History of American Music*. Apparently congregations had been singing whatever approximation of the tune they wanted and the resultant sound was "miserably tortured, and twisted," according to one Roxbury, Massachusetts, minister quoted by Cooke. "I have observed in many Places," the minister continued, "one Man is upon this Note, while another is a Note before him, which produces something so hideous and disorderly, as is beyond Expression bad."

In the schools they were taught to read and sing the hymns as written. Some churches also began appointing one or more of the singers to set the starting note and lead the congregation. It wasn't long before the singing-school graduates became eager for something more. They wanted to perform. So the churches let them sing one Psalm. Then they started seating the singers together. Over time, the graduates started singing songs that were too hard for the congregation to follow. Little by little, and not without resistance, the congregation went from singing to listening. (The debate continued to erupt from time to time, however, and articles about it appeared periodically in local newspapers.)

While the singers were perfecting their craft, a few more composers came along who were hard at work on pieces that would have made St. Augustine gloriously miserable. They were people such as Johann Sebastian Bach, Joseph Haydn, and Wolfgang Amadeus Mozart. Their phenomenal output only fueled the singers' desire for still more chances to indulge this almost unsurpassable pleasure.

The nineteenth century is when we come to the golden age of choral singing. America had sufficiently invested in the infrastructure of a growing nation that it could afford to turn its attention to art and entertainment, and it entered a cultural craze. The cities were first. In New York one cultural institution after another came into being; the Philharmonic Society of New York was founded in 1842; The Metropolitan Museum of Art in 1870; The Metropolitan Opera Association in 1880; Carnegie Hall went up in 1891; and in 1896 Columbia University created a music studies program. The world kept changing in ways that only contributed to the growing popularity of singing. There was the population explosion and particularly the growth of the middle class, and the fact that by the 1830s it was okay for middle-class American women to study music. Music education continued to be introduced and to expand in the schools.

The craze was further fueled when, early in the nineteenth century, music publishers such as Novello started producing small, affordable editions of choral favorites (which usually came down to Handel, Haydn, Mozart, and Beethoven, and later, Mendelssohn and Brahms). The largest contributing factor, however, was America's immigrants. Singing societies had already begun to proliferate in England, Germany, Austria, and elsewhere, and America's most recent settlers, particularly those from Germany, helped spread singing societies, which were all over the cities, to smaller towns in the Northeast, the South, and the Midwest. The railroads being laid down across the states smoothed the way. In the remote Dakota Territory, six months before it was split up into North and South Dakota and admitted into the Union, the city of Yankton hosted a performance of Handel's *Messiah*. By making it easier for singers to travel to choral festivals, the spreading railroads helped build a nationwide choral community.

In the end, singing was simply the most democratic and accessible entry point to great art as a participant, and choral societies became *the* outlet for amateurs to sing and perform. "In no other art are amateurs privileged to enjoy the spiritual beauties of a creation in the degree that music offers to choristers," wrote music critic Henry Edward Krehbiel in 1884. He may have had a problem with all-female singing groups, but he loved choral societies in general. "Whoever belongs to a singing society in which the study is well conducted," he went on, ". . . accomplishes a work and receives an artistic reward analogous to that of the painter who has copied a masterpiece."

"You get to ride on the genius of a Beethoven or a Palestrina," Dimitra Kessenides, an alto in our Choral Society, once raved to me. Dimitra, like others in the Choral Society, joined our group following 9/11. She'd sung in choirs when she was younger but had stopped when her school days were over. "It wasn't until the fall of 2001, living in a wounded, post-9/11 New York City, mourning so many things," she wrote on her blog, "that I finally found my way back to music—cautiously, at first, because I was afraid to count on recapturing past pleasures," but eventually, "I gave in to the music, and the music helped me find my way to a new community, and a new sense of my place in it."

The 9/11 workers themselves felt compelled to sing. One night during the recovery effort, I was helping serve meals down at St. Paul's Chapel when one of the soot-covered rescue workers sitting in the pews looked up at the ceiling and started to sing. I don't recall the song, something properly respectful. But everyone froze. Volunteers stopped pouring coffee and scooping pasta onto dishes, and men paused with food halfway to their mouths. Fires were burning yards away, so close you could smell exactly what was burning down there, and all through the day and night, the following scene played out: the church would be relatively quiet as the workers ate or slept, and then suddenly the firemen's shoulder mics would go off. There'd be a tremendous rustling and banging as all the men jumped to their feet, grabbed their gear, and quickly left the church. A body or a body part had been found. Everyone was on 24-hour death-call alert, knowing that at any moment they'd have to retrieve some precious but mangled piece of flesh—and in the midst of that wretched vigil this guy was singing. No one knew how to respond. We all just stood there like statues, looking at each other for cues. Was this okay? Slowly we all unclenched and listened. Upstairs in the galleries some men cried. Soon after, volunteer musicians began showing up daily to play instruments or sing. The music wasn't always solemn. Diane Reiners, one of the volunteer coordinators, remembers when Sister Helena Marie sat down at the piano and played Jerry Lee Lewis's song "Great Balls of Fire." I personally remember a lot of Sinatra.

It is really no wonder that, once introduced, singing societies spread as quickly as they did. Krehbiel lists eighty-six choral societies nationwide (and a few in Canada) in an 1890 essay, and he was only including the famous ones. There were actually countless more. In 1895 one New York directory alone listed more than ninety "Musical Societies." The Handel and Haydn Society of Boston, which was founded in 1815, continues today. Even the professionals joined in. At one point or another during the nineteenth century, around the world, composers such as Richard Strauss, Johannes Brahms, Anton Bruckner, Robert Schumann, Josef Rheinberger, and Antonín Dvořák were all conducting choral societies. Choral societies became the vehicle for introducing the general public to great sacred and secular music.

All during the nineteenth century, composers continued to crank out piece after piece of immeasurable beauty. They were writing for audiences more and congregations less, and their secular work was influencing what they were writing for the church. Music had reached what is called the romantic period, and trends that had begun in the seventeenth century were now in full force: everything was more operatic, expressive, and emotionally evocative—the kinds of pieces choristers could pour their hearts into. Composers continued to explore the boundaries of what the voice could do, coming up with new harmonies, and for singers and audiences alike it was a musical roller-coaster ride that they wished would never end. In some ways it never has. Pieces like Felix Mendelssohn's *Elijah* (1846), Brahms's *A German Requiem* (finished in 1868), Beethoven's *Missa Solemnis* (1823), and countless others are in many choirs' repertoires today. Three hundred years after people were butchering hymns in church, I'm still singing Handel's *Messiah*. And if it's the spring, I'm singing the Brahms *Requiem,* or Mozart's *Requiem,* or the Duruflé or Verdi *Requiem;* the point is, in the spring we sing about death.

It's not a problem for me, I have always been drawn to the subject of death. I'm not morbid, exactly. Death terrifies me. But more information has always equaled less terror; therefore, I think, talk, and write about death. A lot. One spring at the beginning of rehearsal John said, "And now we sing about death," and the tenor next to me said, "Oh, this is your song."

Conveniently for me, death is among every choir's greatest hits. One of the earliest written musical compositions was by a twelfth-century French composer named Pérotin, and it consisted of one word only: *Mors.* "Death." So it was a spring song. I imagine a bunch of monks intoning death, death, death, death, death, death, death, when all around them the cherry blossoms bloomed, or whatever flowers grew back then in the gardens where they were cloistered. But they had to be getting something out of it.

In many ways we're still singing what the monks were chanting all those centuries ago. In some cases we're singing the exact same thing, what has become the standard or ordinary choral mass. It's essentially a musical setting of a traditional religious service, and it's made up of the following sections: the Kyrie, Gloria, Credo, Sanctus, Benedictus, and Agnus Dei. Most classical composers have taken a crack at the mass, and they have done so whether they believe in God or not. Week after week, year after year I'm singing some line like, "We praise you, we bless you, we adore you, we glorify you," and I'm perfectly fine with the fact that I do none of those things. When I was younger it was more important to me to let it be known to everyone that I do not praise, bless, adore, or glorify that guy who by the way does not exist. Gentle images of St. Francis of Assisi, with birds coming to rest on his outstretched hands, so irresistible to an animal-loving child, had been quickly obliterated by the ring of angry red faces of the adults I can still see above me, whenever I dared question something from the Bible.

But now I can't help but be grateful that religion has inspired and paid for what is arguably the most beautiful work our species has ever produced. I still have moments of disconnect, like when we sing, "O death where is thy sting, o grave where is thy victory?" *Right*. But I choose to focus on the beauty of the music and on lyrics that I can relate to, such as "Ye shall have a song and gladness of heart." Even though God is not the answer for me, the music written in His name is. It both eases whatever pain I am suffering from and heightens all my joys. While it sometimes feels as if religion only separates people, the music brings us together.

"This is church for me," fellow choir member alto Peggy Willens once said me. Soprano Lucia Rivieccio agreed. "If anything is God-like it's singing; it surrounds you with love, friendship, comfort, beauty, and there is a soaring feeling, maybe it's a soprano thing but in certain pieces I feel like I'm flying." "I consider singing my form of prayer," echoed another chorister. But soprano Christina Davis best summed up what I feel. "I am an agnostic verging on an atheist, but find that sacred music is not antithetical to my beliefs (in the way that sitting through a church service is). I've come to the conclusion that music alone (and not the liturgy) represents the essence of what I would find palatable and comforting in religion. When I sing or listen to sacred music I feel a primal, essential proximity of my fellow man; I feel that the word 'god' is just a great Vowel surrounded by two consonants, something essentially open and going-forth. I can fathom others' faith only through music: If, as Buckminster Fuller once said, 'God is a verb,' that verb is singing."

Ralph Vaughan Williams, one of my favorite composers, did not believe in God, and yet he spent two years editing an English hymnal, a revised version of which is still in use today. "Although a declared agnostic," his second wife, Ursula, wrote, "he was able, all through his life, to set to music words in the accepted terms of Christian revelation as if they meant to him what they must have meant to George Herbert or to Bunyan" (religious writers whose words Vaughan Williams set to music).

Ralph Vaughan Williams is also the source of one of my favorite quotes about amateur singing. "If we want to find the groundwork of our English culture we must look below the surface—not to the grand events chronicled in the newspapers but . . . to the village choral societies whose members trudge miles through rain and snow to work steadily for a concert or competition in some ghastly parish room with a cracked piano and a smelly oil lamp where one week there is no tenor because at best there are only two, and one has a cold and the other being the village doctor is always called out at the critical moment; and there they sit setting their teeth so as to wrench the heart out of this mysterious piece of music which they are starting to learn . . ."

Until John Maclay took over our choir I'd never heard of Ralph Vaughan Williams, and I didn't particularly like him at first. I can pick up a Mozart piece I've never heard before and even if I get half the notes wrong and someone near me is loudly tapping out their own personal rhythm and the entire choir is managing only the barest approximation of what the piece is supposed to sound like, I can still tell how extraordinary it's going to be. The first Ralph Vaughan Williams piece we did took some time to appreciate, and even then I had my doubts. When John announced that we were going to do an all–Vaughan Williams concert I thought, wasn't there a Mozart piece we hadn't done yet? Then we ran through "Toward the Unknown Region."

The text is from "Darest Thou Now, O Soul," a Walt Whitman poem. Even though in the bottom of my heart I think there is nothing! nothing! nothing! after death, by the time we get to the very last chords I've been sucked in. In spite of a lifetime of disbelief, for a few moments I let go and allow myself to hope that what I always thought would be the worst moment in my life could go another way.

Darest thou now, O soul,

Walk out with me toward the unknown region,

Where neither ground is for the feet, nor any path to follow?

No map there, nor guide,

Nor voice sounding, nor touch of human hand,

Nor face with blooming flesh, nor lips, nor eyes, are in that
   land.

I know it not O soul,

Nor dost thou, all is a blank before us,

All waits undreamed of in that region, that inaccessible
   land . . .

Then we burst forth, we float,

In time and space, O soul, prepared for them;

Equal, equipt at last, O joy! O fruit of all! them to fulfil,
   O soul.

The complete absence of fantastic, implausible images of God and Heaven in "Toward the Unknown Region" is thrilling. It makes the suggestion that there's something beyond death that is, if not exactly possible, at least a little less . . . absurd. When the piece was performed at the Leeds Festival in 1907 it was even more revolutionary. "Almost for the first time," Vaughan Williams's biographer Michael Kennedy wrote, "an English festival choir was singing aspiring, liberating words which were not specifically religious, i.e., were not drawn from the Bible." Although Vaughan Williams insisted that searching for specific, concrete meaning and emotion in music was a mistake, "the function of music is to be beautiful and nothing less—it cannot be more," I think that's overstating it. His yearning is unmistakable. When a man in his early thirties writes music about death as if it's the most wonderful thing in the world, I want to know why.

Williams lost his father when he was two years old. While that was tragic and would have caused its own kind of lasting damage, chances are he would have at most a few ghostlike memories. His wife Ursula wrote about how as a young boy he rode home with his family late one winter night in a horse-drawn carriage. As they passed through one small village they heard the sound of a bell tolling. Ralph asked why it rang, and so slowly, and he was told that someone must have died. "So his first realization of death came through a country custom and by means of music." It's a lovely story, but it seems more likely that his first realization would have come when he asked, "Why don't I have a father, like the other boys?"

A better clue is in the piece's dedication. It reads simply "To F. H. M." Florence Henrietta Maitland. Florence was the sister of Ralph's first wife, Adeline, and she had just lost her husband, the professor and historian Frederick Maitland. In his college days, Vaughan Williams spent a lot of time at the Maitlands' house, where he would often form a small chamber group with some of his fellow undergraduates. The young and beautiful Adeline Fisher, who once played for Tchaikovsky, frequently joined in on the cello or the piano. The act of making music together is an intimate, heady experience, and it wasn't long before Ralph proposed. All this blossomed in the Maitlands' drawing room. Ten years later, when Frederick Maitland died while on vacation, Vaughan Williams had the grim task of helping Florence Maitland escort the body of her husband home, to the very place where they all had laughed and sung and where Ralph had fallen in love. He'd been working on "Toward the Unknown Region" for the past year. With the death of his beloved friend and mentor, it would have become suddenly and terribly important that the hope held out in Walt Whitman's poignant words was real.

In a bittersweet twist of fate, "Toward the Unknown Region" would come back forty-five years later and once again link love, death, and music. By this time, the Adeline of those fairy-tale days was long gone. She suffered from a lifetime of debilitating pain caused by rheumatoid arthritis, and had become increasingly disabled. For decades she lived between bed and wheelchair. By all accounts, Vaughan Williams took very tender care of her, carrying her from room to room, never making her feel that he experienced a moment of regret. But the years had taken their toll. In 1938 the sixty-five-year-old Ralph Vaughan Williams met the gorgeous and captivating twenty-seven-year-old Ursula; a few hours later they were stealing kisses in a taxi. Those kisses launched a love affair that would last until the day he died.

On May 10, 1951, Ralph took a train to London to meet Ursula, and together they went to a student choral society rehearsal of "Toward the Unknown Region." Sometime during that performance, Adeline died. When Ralph returned home he'd learn that while he and Ursula were listening to the university students sing "All waits, undreamed of, in that region, that inaccessible land," Adeline was listening to those same words, too. A group of women had huddled around Adeline, singing "Toward the Unknown Region." As she slipped way into that inaccessible land, his first song about death, the piece he had dedicated to her sister all those years ago, had been ringing in both their ears.

Two years after Adeline died, Ursula and Ralph were married. It was a quiet ceremony and no music played. Vaughan Williams was eighty years old now, and he lived on vigorously and passionately for six more years. He composed his last piece, his Ninth Symphony, between 1956 and 1957. Vaughan Williams was nearly deaf by this time, but unlike poor Beethoven, he was able to hear his Ninth performed on August 5, 1958, with the benefit of a hearing aid that looked more like a tiny trumpet. A few weeks later, on August 26, with Ursula by his side, Vaughan Williams had a heart attack and died.

"THE ART OF music," Vaughan Williams wrote, "requires two minds . . . the composer and the performer. If the composer is wise he will not try to make his score foolproof, but will wait for the twin-mind which will translate his imaginings into sound, and consummate that marriage of true minds which alone can give his music life."

There are other ways to be intimate with another human

being, but few that seem to touch something that is so deep within us and is so rarely shared. Singing is the ultimate communion. You're not just listening to the music, but becoming it. It's like a musical seance. You're channeling what the composer was thinking and feeling. When we're singing "Toward the Unknown Region," for a short time the once wildly beating heart of Ralph Vaughan Williams is alive again. His grief in the face of death is reawakened, but so is the path he created to get past pain, fear, and sorrow.

When we arrive at the part in the piece about a place or state where we can no longer look into the eyes of those we love, or hold their hands, where we won't ever be able to laugh or cry or sing again—what could have been a bleak or terrifying section—Vaughan Williams gave us this direction: *misterioso*. He wanted neither fear nor sorrow, but beauty and mystery. That great big question of death, "All is a blank," is incredibly moving in Vaughan Williams's hands. There are no answers here, only questions held out with an open heart. When I sing about that moment, the moment of death, I can hardly wait to die, which is insane. But the music just keeps growing and swelling in emotion and I get swept up. "All waits undreamed of," we sing, all the voice parts coming together, then apart, then entwined again, each enticing step of the vocal dance drawing us deeper into the beautiful mystery where anything is possible. It's not about dying or the afterlife. It's about living for a few seconds in a very open way, without fear, and being a part of something magnificent.

"I have a pocket that I've sewn into my pants for a cough

drop and Kleenex," Peggy Willens told me, and she had to pull out that tissue while we sang "Toward the Unknown Region." For another Choral Society member, singing this particular piece at that particular time was even harder. While we were rehearsing that fall, Christina Davis lost her father to pancreatic cancer. His death was brutally swift and unexpected, and she talked about how bass Tim Bohn had come over to her one night, having just lost his own father. "Tim and I had only spoken once in my entire four- or five-year Grace Church experience, and he said he was concerned for me: 'I don't like to think of you having to sing this right now.' That compassion from him, from an utter stranger in New York City, seemed to typify both the empathic spirit of Whitman and the transcendental capacity of that particular piece of music."

Death was all around us that year, so much so that John titled our program a Concert for Peace. We were waging two wars with no end in sight and there was talk of still more conflicts. But John e-mailed us that he meant peace, not just in the "literal, immediate sense (though we all devoutly wish it), but the peace that comes from knowing that through all its tortured ages, and even from the depths of war and all its carnage, human beings have an innate capacity for reconciliation, the spine to stand up to tyranny, and an ability to seek out the 'new heavens and the new earth' that lie beyond. Armies can be defeated; human beings—soldiers, civilians—cannot. The first step to ending a war is to remember what peace feels like.

These voices—yours, and those we read from—are powerful reminders."

That spring I came across a wounded pigeon huddled on its side by a wheel of a car. I tried to walk on. *People are dying everywhere all over the world. I walk by homeless people every day, and I am going to stop now and assist . . . a pigeon?* I looked around. Not only would no one help me, most people would be angry at me for trying. "Flying rats," they'd mutter. I made it two blocks. But I knew that for the rest of my life whenever I was filled with self-loathing my mind would go straight to "Remember that hurt pigeon you left to die in the gutter?" I went back. I looked down and tried to will myself not to feel. But here was this poor, turned-over, splayed, shivering creature who at that moment was desperately trying to hide from the world and death and whatever pain it was feeling by dragging itself farther underneath the car. For months I'd been singing about the fear we feel when we lose the ground beneath our feet, and I knew some pigeon-equivalent feeling must have been racing through his sorry, scared little pigeon heart.

I got a box from a jewelry store, then called a friend who cursed me but agreed to Google "pigeon rescue New York." A few hours later I was in the home of a pigeon first responder, who turned out to be B-movie actress and fifties pin-up girl Meg Myles, star of *Satan in High Heels*. She handled my pigeon expertly, got him drinking and eating, and a few days later she called to tell me that though he'd been hit by a car and had a broken leg and wing, he'd be okay, pigeons heal quickly. They had set his breaks, fed him, and within in a week he'd be heading up to a bird sanctuary, where he'd live out his days with plenty of food and water and be safe from indifferent, barreling cars.

I felt so ridiculously happy. All that death that year, but I'd had one tiny victory. A few months later I was one of the people chosen to read names on the anniversary of 9/11. Every year a different group of people is selected to read the names of all the people who died on September 11, 2001. That year, volunteers and first responders were the designated group and I was among them. I was given nine names. Nine people who were going about their business when the ground gave way beneath their feet. As Whitman wrote and Vaughan Williams set to music, "No map there, nor guide, Nor voice sounding, nor touch of human hand . . ." Death always wins.

VAUGHAN WILLIAMS ONCE said to a group of school children, "Music will enable you to see past facts to the very essence of things in a way which science cannot do. The arts are the means by which we can look through the magic casements and see what lies beyond." That's what those monks were after when they chanted death, death, death, death, death. They weren't being morbid. They weren't ignoring the beauty all around them. They were trying to understand something they couldn't fathom in any other way. "Toward the Unknown Region" is Ralph Vaughan Williams's death chant, his answer to the eternal silence.

For someone who believes that death always wins, and that

there is nothing beyond that inescapable end, music is one of the few answers that I can accept. A member of conductor Robert Shaw's choir told him that every time he sings the Bach *Mass in B Minor* he is "conscious of the fact that someone in the audience is hearing it for the first time, and someone is hearing it for the last time." I have thoughts like that, too. But every once in a while when I sing I also think that one of these days it will be my last. Someday I will leave this church after a performance or a rehearsal and never come back again.

That day came in 2008 for one of our basses, Frits Menschaar. Frits was eighty years old and he died during the spring, when we were, as usual, singing about death. Among the last words Frits sang were, "I tremble and fear at the coming desolation and wrath. Day of wrath, calamity and misery, great and exceedingly bitter day." Thankfully, we were also working on Mendelssohn's *Jauchzet dem Herrn,* so he would have also sung, "Make a joyful noise unto the Lord, all ye lands. Serve the Lord with gladness: come before his presence with song." At the next rehearsal, a few days after Frits died, John asked us to remember Frits as we sang in his honor the final movement from another piece we'd been rehearsing for the spring, the Duruflé *Requiem.*

In paradisum deducant te Angeli:
in tuo adventu suscipiant te martyres,
et perducant te in civitatem sanctam Jerusalem.
Chorus angelorum te suscipiat,
et cum Lazaro quondam paupere æternam habeas requiem.

Which translates to:

> May Angels lead you into paradise;
> may the Martyrs receive you at your coming
> and lead you to the holy city of Jerusalem.
> May a choir of Angels receive you,
> and with Lazarus, who once was poor, may you have
>   eternal rest.

I didn't know our bass Frits Menschaar very well. For decades we sat on opposite sides of the room at rehearsals. But Howard Place, a fellow bass, told me that Frits, who grew up in Nazi-occupied Holland, sometimes subsisting on one or two potatoes a week, was a member of several singing groups around the city. The week before he died, Frits had attended choir rehearsals on Monday, Tuesday, Wednesday, and Thursday. So I know at least one thing about Frits that had to have been true: even though he was singing about death, in the spring, right before dying himself, he wouldn't have wanted it any other way. "He was doing what he loved until the very end," choir member Wendy Hayden agreed. We can wish him into paradise all we want, but I know that he's already been there. A lot.

A couple of days after performing the Vaughan Williams piece, I wrote on my blog, "I can't believe this season is over." I loved the music so much I couldn't believe that was it. "I want to do it again," I said.

Those are going to be my words on my death bed. "I want to do it again."

Recitative
The People's Choral Union

1892 was a tough year for the working class in New York. One poor slob was indicted that year for "receiving stolen goods," a felony charge, even though the stolen goods in this particular case were nothing more than fourteen bunches of bananas. Another was arrested for trying to stay warm by stealing a blanket off a horse. It was such a short fall to rock bottom. On September 16, a man named Andrew Stewart jumped from the Washington Bridge into the dark brown waters of the Harlem River below. When a workman rushed over and pulled him out, Stewart said he took the dive because he was unable support his wife and children and he couldn't bear to see them suffer.

For the garment workers, clerks, and shop girls barely keeping it together, there wasn't a lot of money left over for art or leisure. Frank Damrosch was lucky enough to have none of these problems. He'd come to America from Germany in 1871 when he was twelve years old, and it wasn't long before his father, conductor Leopold Damrosch, had successfully recreated the world of beauty and music they'd left back home. The Oratorio Society of New York he founded is still around today, along with the New York Symphony Society, which he also created and which would later merge with the Philharmonic Society of New York to become the world-famous New York Philharmonic.

Although Frank had made a stab at independence and had gone into business, he was ultimately unable to resist the lure of the musical life that had always surrounded him. It wasn't long before he was working as the chorus master at the Metropolitan Opera and conducting the Mendelssohn Glee Club. Despite having a charmed life, he was always keenly aware of the struggle around him. "The greatest giver of comfort and happiness in life" was music, he said, and notes were "the key to the storehouse." He couldn't help noticing that only the well-to-do held those keys—the musicians and singers in the societies he belonged to weren't stealing blankets off horses. "Think," he said, "what music means to the poor man and woman whose lives are hampered by the material questions of existence," and then contrast that with "the wealthy who have more music offered to them than they can digest. . . ." Frank Damrosch wanted to give the working men and women of New York City their own set of keys to the storehouse. In 1892, when he was only thirty-three years old, he started the People's Singing Classes.

He scheduled a demonstration for October 23 at Cooper Union, the same place where, seventeen years later, thousands of factory workers would vote to strike, hoping to eliminate the conditions that eventually led to the Triangle Shirtwaist Factory fire of 1911. Damrosch distributed flyers for his event and then waited, worrying that no one would come. On the day of the event an immense crowd stood waiting outside on the street. Twenty-five hundred men and women had shown up in a hall that was built to hold seven hundred. Damrosch gave the people inside their first sight-singing lesson, then the audience was switched out with the people on the street and Damrosch did the whole thing again. At the end of each demonstration "self-supporting men of eighteen and over and women of fifteen and over" were invited to sign up for his classes. The charge was ten cents per class ($2.50 in 2012 dollars). The response was so great that Damrosch had to scramble to open additional classes around Manhattan and the outer boroughs.

At the first official class, Damrosch taught everyone the round "Oh How Lovely Is the Evening," and then he separated the singers into three groups. No one wanted to begin. It was just barely okay when they were all singing in unison. And everyone was afraid that when it was their turn to enter, they'd get it wrong. But Frank Damrosch was the Atticus Finch of conductors. He had a calm, fatherly manner, and within minutes he got the first group to begin, then the second, and finally the third. The effect was dazzling. "They straggled out" afterwards, wrote Damrosch biographer Lucy Poate Stebbins, forever changed by their success. Word got out, more people were signing up for classes, and soon Damrosch was challenging the growing student body to ever more difficult pieces.

Before long, thousands of working men and women were mastering pieces by Handel, Mendelssohn, and others. But Frank wanted his choristers to have the same opportunity other singers had once they learned a piece of music: the chance to perform. The first concert for the newly established People's Choral Union was at the also relatively new Carnegie Hall, which had gone up only two years before and was built in part due to his brother, Walter's, influence with Andrew Carnegie. People's Choral Union concerts at Carnegie Hall were to become a yearly tradition, often with over a thousand singers crowding the stage and the orchestra below. After attending a concert in 1900, Louis Comfort Tiffany wrote in a letter that the concert master Damrosch had "changed Carnegie Hall into a grand cathedral." Henry Edward Krehbiel, the *New York Tribune* music critic who had been so hard on the Rubinstein Club, said the People's Choral Union concerts had "genuine musical value," and that the concert he'd attended had created "a truly thrilling effect seldom presented as the composer intended."

By then there were twenty-seven People's Singing Classes in New York, and People's Choral Unions in New Jersey, Boston, Pennsylvania, Rhode Island, and Canada. Roofers and plasterers would sometimes stop Damrosch in the street to thank him. One man ran off to get his well-worn and much marked Handel score to illustrate the story he proceeded to proudly tell. He was a school janitor and the father of six children, he said. Even though he was working a second job, he couldn't afford the music education he wanted his children to have. Then he heard about the Choral Union. Now he was taking classes and teaching his children what he'd learned.

In a 1902 letter to the editor of the *New York Times,* one audience member expressed his displeasure about something he'd witnessed at one of their concerts. "I like to see their splendid enthusiasm," he wrote,"but I think it is woefully out of place for them to show it by applauding the conductor when he first comes on. . . . If they wish to be taken seriously they must act seriously. Let them applaud Mr. Damrosch at rehearsals as much as they choose, but he should discourage all such kindergarten displays in a public concert. . . . It is utterly ridiculous for them to applaud a programme of which they are a part."

The author of the letter had failed to comprehend the depth of the singers' gratitude. Long after Damrosch retired, and many years after he had taught his last People's Singing Class, his former students presented him with a poem written in his honor. It described the cold, unfriendly world outside, and the hall in the basement where they held their classes, with gas jets that were often leaking, and pillars that blocked their view, but, "Those hours shaped again and again, / Your life, your very soul, / In ways you'd not comprehend / . . . You took the blue from out the skies, / And sparkles from the stars, / And bound them, / In Heaven's grandest harmonies." For the rest of Damrosch's life his students sent him a box of roses every year on his birthday, one flower for each year of his life.

In 1918 Damrosch received a letter from Richard Fletcher, the editor of a newspaper called *The Chronicle*. Fletcher had just published an editorial by Mrs. William Jay, the only woman on the board of directors at the New York Philharmonic. It was the last year of World War I, and a nationwide push to ban all German music had begun. Mrs. Jay's editorial called on all the great musical institutions of New York to join the ban. Many prominent people in the musical world, including John Philip Sousa, were in favor of the ban, and Fletcher wanted Damrosch to write something in support.

It's hard to imagine that Fletcher actually thought Damrosch, a German American, might comply. The very first piece the New York Philharmonic had ever performed was composed by Beethoven. German American musicians, conductors, and composers and Damrosch's own father had helped make the Philharmonic the important musical institution it was and remains today. German immigrants were largely responsible for the proliferation of choral societies throughout the United States, introducing Americans to music they would otherwise not have heard for many decades. In his book *The German Element in the United States,* Prof. Albert Bernhard Faust writes, "The thesis may be maintained without hesitation, that the Germans are responsible for the development of musical tastes in the United States." Although I might modify that slightly to "largely responsible," there is no question that America is musically in debt to our German immigrants.

And now Fletcher was asking the man whose German American family had so enriched the musical life of New York City that Lincoln Center would later name a park in their honor, to join him in a ban of some of the world's great composers.

In his response, Damrosch manages to be both patient and condemning. "Why deprive ourselves of the things that are good and beautiful at a time when the world cannot have too much of just such things?" he wrote.

> I refuse to believe that the American people are so unintelligent as to be unable to distinguish between the German militaristic government and Beethoven's music, or that they would cease to hate the former because they love the latter. It is so silly a contention that one wonders that supposedly intelligent people can utter or believe it.
>
> In my opinion American patriotism should express itself by living up to American ideals of freedom. . . . German militarism will not be defeated by the exclusion of the masterworks of German music. . . . Nor will it be defeated by the persecution of harmless German artists, nor by efforts to incite a mob-spirit against works of art which have nothing to do with German autocracy or militarism. . . . Let us preserve our dignity and fairness and appreciation of what is true, beautiful and noble. . . .

(Where was someone like Frank Damrosch in 2003, when members of our Congress declared that french fries would now be called "freedom fries?")

The People's Singing Classes disbanded in 1917. Damrosch included singing classes for the people in a proposal for a music complex that he presented to the board of the Institute of Musical Art, which he cofounded (and which later merged with the Juilliard Graduate School to form what is now the world-famous Juilliard School of Music), but his plan was not adopted. Frank Damrosch retired in 1933 and died in 1937, when he was seventy-eight years old.

Although Damrosch's name and contributions are largely forgotten outside of scholarly circles, an estimated fifty thousand people learned to sing because of Frank Damrosch. A financial backer of his would say of his achievements, "It is a beautiful thing and a rare one, to have a real ideal. It is rarer still to find it possible to make this ideal a living thing, and still rarer to convert it into one that will continue to live when all of us will be gone."

Almost a decade after Damrosch died, a former People's Singing Classes student wrote, "Classical music did not come into my life until about 1892." He'd been a young and struggling law student at the time and had some access to music, but "the door to great things in music was not really opened for me until that year, when Frank Damrosch opened it wide for thousands, of which fortunately, I chanced to be one. . . . Dr. Frank is our own hero," he wrote. "He was our friend."

Mass No. 11 in D Minor, *aka* Missa in Angustiis

Written by Joseph Haydn in 1798

Performed by the Choral Society of Grace Church in the Winter, 2010

Something was wrong. We couldn't pinpoint where the problem was, exactly, but somewhere within the choir the timing was just enough off-kilter that all the vocal parts had started to veer away from each other. If we could have, we would simply have stopped singing and started over, but a churchful of people were watching. Instead, the choir began to react, each section confident for a split second that their tempo was the correct one, which made matters worse. The clear, brilliant sound we had been making was starting to sound ever so slightly muddy. It took only another second for whatever confidence remained to melt away. Now the orchestra was picking up on the wall of wrongness behind them, and their timing was perceptibly beginning to slide. Or maybe we heard it that way because we were off. That's when our

voices started to clash. Two seconds later and we were sounding a little like that noise DJs make when they're scrubbing a
record. We were in free fall, just moments away from complete
catastrophe. *Don't look horrified, don't look horrified, keep a
straight face.*

"It's like the whole room was spinning," Brent Whitman
recalled. "You're really not sure which way is up, or straight,
or whatever." "I remember standing in the back," Christina
Davis said, "and suddenly feeling like I was singing alone on
my part and then it all sort of went blank. I was terrified." All
season long John had been imploring us, "Once in a while
remember that you have a conductor! Get your faces out of the
music and look at me!" Our faces were out of our music now.
Fear leapt from the heart of one chorister to the next, like
thoughts jumping between synaptic connections in a brain.
All 145 members of the choir were looking to John, every pair
of eyes crying *Fix this.*

John didn't look the least bit alarmed; his expression had
all the focus and intensity of a music-traffic controller. He was
going to land this baby. "Don't worry," he once said, when
asked how he was going to give us a cut-off. "I'll use signal
flags." Right now what we needed was his pulse, the simple up
and down movement of his baton, which as of that moment
we were following to the absolute rhythmical second. *Trust the
baton.* In one gloriously unified moment of attention, everything snapped back into place. The bright, sparkling clarity of
rhythmic perfection returned and the wave of panic that had

briefly arisen throughout the choir just as quickly subsided. I'm sure the audience never even noticed. John was pointing to his baton. Okay, now he looked a little mad.

He forgave us soon after. Before one of the most dramatic sections in the piece, while his right arm continued to mark time, he held out his left hand, with his fingers curled together in a tight fist, meaning "hold it, hold it, don't let go yet." As he slowly lifted his arm, we matched him with an increase in volume and force. At the same time, the violins were dashing up and down, going impossibly fast and perfectly around the line we were singing, the trumpets punctuating to the left, the timpani pounding to the right. When his arm could go no higher John spread all his fingers up and out as if to say, "Now! Let loose your hearts NOW." It was like they'd burst from us. Everyone in the audience sat up taller in their seats. The oboe player in front of me turned around and smiled. John tilted his head back, his face brightening as it caught the light from the chandeliers, then he half-closed his eyes and started swaying, his expression pure bliss.

The psychologist Gerhart Harrer once ran a series of physiological tests on the German conductor Herbert von Karajan, who also happened to be—speaking of landings—a pilot. Harrer measured and compared Karajan's heartbeat while conducting the Berlin Philharmonic to his heartbeat while flying and executing what are called "touch and goes." Touch and goes are a method of practicing takeoffs and landings. You come in for a landing and barely touch down before heading right back off into the wild blue yonder in order to circle back and do it all again. It's a potentially dangerous maneuver, which recently caused the death of a student pilot. But I was a student pilot years ago and the truth is that touch and goes are also like being on the best roller coaster in the world. Yet the whole time during the maneuver Karajan's heart rate never went above 115 beats per minute. However, 115 was merely his average while conducting Beethoven's *Leonore* overture. During the most emotional moment in the piece Karajan's heart rate hurtled up to 150. I'm guessing our rhythmic crisis elicited barely a rise in John's pulse but it soared in the section where he released his fingers and set our voices free.

Over the next ninety minutes, a masterpiece came to life without a single word being spoken. After the concert, an audience member came up to me and asked, "Do you really need a conductor up there? I mean, you all know the music, don't you? What do you need him for?"

For the longest time choirs didn't have conductors as we know them today. Even as late as the nineteenth century, choral conducting was still relatively new. According to Robert Jourdain in *Music, the Brain, and Ecstasy,* conductors once wandered about the choir whispering instructions. After orchestras joined the choir, it became customary for a violinist to lead one section while the harpsichordist led another. Mozart was so unhappy with how the orchestra rehearsed his *Paris Symphony* that he considered skipping the performance altogether. "I finally resolved to go," he wrote his father, "with the

proviso that if things went as ill as at the rehearsal I would certainly make my way into the orchestra, snatch Herr Lahouse's
instrument from his hand and conduct myself!" (Lahouse was
the first violinist.) During opera performances, the conductor
would stand discreetly off to the side, pounding a staff into
the floor. In the early nineteenth century when conductors
first stood before the orchestra and choir, they faced the audience and not the musicians, so as not to appear rude; and they
brandished rolled-up sheets of paper and not a baton. There
are competing claims about who was first to wield an actual
baton, but scholars seem to agree that Felix Mendelssohn is
largely responsible for popularizing its use beginning in 1829.

Mendelssohn is also often credited with being a key figure
in expanding and defining the conductor's role. Descriptions
of his style are quite florid. "When once his fine, firm hand
grasped the baton, the electric fire of his soul seemed to stream
out through it, and was felt at once by singers, orchestra and
audience," Wilhelm Adolf Lampadius writes in his *Life of
Felix Mendelssohn*. During this period, conductors went from
being little more than a human metronome to virtuosos of the
highly technical art form conducting is today. They'd taken
charge. The final sound that was produced was their responsibility now.

"So, PEOPLE SLEEPING with their sisters," John was
saying, "that's basically the whole Ring thing." *What the hell?*
I'm so easily distracted. It's a middle-age thing. We can still

generate brain cells and white matter, and according to the results of one long-term study, in some very key tests such as verbal memory and inductive reasoning, we perform better than twenty-five-year-olds. But our minds wander. John had been explaining something about Wagner's *Ring Cycle* one season, and I'm sorry I missed it, because everyone was laughing. Another time I came back from daydreaming and John was saying, "This is the part in the piece where everyone is coming up out of the ground incorruptible and you're singing it like accountants." Someday he'll tell everyone to sing a normally *forte* (loud) section *pianissimo* (as softly as possible) and I'll be the only voice bellowing out at the concert, because at the precise moment he gave that instruction I was thinking about what was on TV.

Tonight was our first rehearsal after a four-month-long break (it was September and our last concert was in May; we have concerts in December and April or May). We were anxious to sing some notes, any notes at all. We warmed up, ran briefly through one of the pieces we were going to perform, and when John called out "Welcome to choir!" afterward, our relief was so great we burst into applause, only I was worrying about veterinary bills. One of my cats was suffering through some very expensive medical issues that I didn't have the money to pay for. I'd been in debt once in my life and I swore I'd never go into debt again, but what choice did I have? I started putting the bills on a credit card. I looked down at my music and noticed for the first time that I was having trouble reading my music and seeing John at the same time. I needed bifocals. *Terrific. More money, more debt. Plus, I'm old.*

John was checking a piece of paper. After introducing all the new people—at which point I quickly scanned them, in vain, for a new man my age—he started talking about the piece we were going to feature that December, a Haydn mass. I'm always curious to hear what John has to say about his choices. With roughly six centuries of music to choose from and a ton of people clamoring for their favorites, why this piece, why now?

"Haydn is the whole reason I'm here," he began. The first choral piece he'd ever sung was a Haydn mass, when he was twelve years old. "I was hooked." Ah. No one ever forgets their first love. "I think that Haydn's last six masses are among the highest achievements in Western music," John explained, and they were all on his "must do" list. We'd already done the *Mass in Time of War*, so the *Mass no. 11 in D* was next. It's known as the *Lord Nelson* Mass, after Admiral Horatio Nelson, who defeated Napoleon in a key battle in 1798, the year the mass was written (Nelson may have attended an early performance). Haydn actually titled it *Missa in Angustiis*, and that's been translated as the *Mass for Troubled Times* or *Strained Times* or *Straitened Times*. Bottom line, not the best of times.

I can see why John chose this particular piece now. We're still at war; our economy has yet to recover. While struggling to come up with ways to earn money, I came across an article listing "10 Careers with High Rates of Depression." Artists, entertainers, and writers were among the ten. *Of course.* "These jobs can bring irregular paychecks, uncertain hours, and isolation," the piece read. I burst into tears. Money was so tight that I took down a bird feeder I'd put up on my fire escape only the summer before to save forty dollars a month. I was getting mostly pigeons, but I was fine with that. Ever since the pigeon rescue incident, pigeons and I have a thing. Except the pigeons heartbreakingly continued to show up long after the feeder was gone. They'd walk right up to the window and stare at me, patiently waiting for food that would never come again.

The year Haydn wrote his mass, 1798, was likewise a rough year; it was yet another rough year following a great long stretch of difficult years, and people were weary. The world was financially and politically unstable. (Over in America we'd just passed four Alien and Sedition Acts.) Napoleon was still at it and heading eastward. On a more personal note, Haydn, like Vaughan Williams, had a wife who suffered from crippling arthritis. He was tired, overextended, but after having just put a lid on another composition, *The Creation,* he was expected to immediately get to work on a mass to be performed on the name day of the wife of his employer, Nikolaus II, Prince Esterhazy. However, due to the preparations for the first performance of *The Creation,* Haydn got a late start and he now had only two months left. To make matters worse, in an effort to save some money, Nikolaus had just fired the entire wind section of the orchestra. Music costs. Between the church and the court, someone had to pay for all this beauty. Make do, the prince must have said to Haydn.

Haydn was earning a respectable living, but he was feeling the effects of the economy, too. The year before, he'd written the prince's administrator to complain about having to pay a relative's debts. "I swear by the Kyrie eleison which I am at this moment supposed to compose for my fourth Prince [Haydn had worked for earlier princes in the Esterhazy family] . . . I have fallen into the same state of insolvency . . . but with the difference that he has fallen from his horse to the back of an ass, whilst I have managed to remain on the horse, but without saddle or harness." Haydn was stressed.

In the end, it took him fifty-three days. He had nine days left before the deadline, but he still had to write out all the parts, rehearse the chorus, the soloists, and finally the orchestra, such as it was. He didn't make it. The first performance was two weeks after the princess's name day. Still, not bad for a tired and overextended sixty-six-year-old.

Two hundred twelve years later, while preparing to put on this very same mass, John Maclay was dealing with some of the same issues. Music still costs. Like everything else, the expense of keeping a choir has gone up considerably. Part of the reason is size. Medieval and Renaissance choirs were small; if you had twenty-five singers, that was considered a huge choir. Haydn, for instance, had about eight singers to think about when he was getting ready to put on the

Lord Nelson Mass. We were going to have 152. The orchestra affects the cost even more. For centuries, this wasn't even a consideration. Instruments to accompany the singers simply weren't allowed inside the church and all singing was a cappella. By the 1100s, however, organs had become acceptable and it was only a matter of time before every church had to have one. (In New York the first organ was installed in a church in 1724.) Slowly other instruments were added, driving the costs ever higher, until we get to today, when no one thinks twice about seeing a full-blown orchestra inside a church.

As I write this, unemployment is near 10 percent, the economy is a mess, people are losing their houses, millions can't afford health insurance, and I can't pay for eyeglasses or bird seed. Operating expenses for the Choral Society of Grace Church have reached $100,000 to $120,000 a season. (A choral year is referred to as the season, and for us that lasts from September to May. The periods within the season are called semesters. So we have winter and spring semesters.) Those already substantial costs are going to be even higher this year while Grace Church undergoes a major restoration and we have to rent space elsewhere for our December concert. Love may be one factor in selecting music, but the other is money. Big pieces such as Beethoven's *Missa Solemnis* or the Duruflé *Requiem*, which require a large orchestra, can cost as much as $40,000 to $50,000 to stage, while a cappella pieces are considerably less. By firing the wind section over two hundred years ago, Prince Nikolaus II saved us $5,000 thousand dollars today, but it's still going to be an expensive year. In addition to the space issue, John has an ambitious program planned for the spring. Where does money like that come from in this economy?

CHOIRMASTER BRUCE MCINNES retired midway through the term in 1999, when John Maclay was thirty-one years old and the Choral Society's assistant conductor. While the church was scrambling to find interim directors for each of the four choirs McInnes was currently overseeing—the boys' choir, the girls' choir, the adult choir, and finally the Choral Society—John was making plans to jump on the chance to direct the Choral Society himself. He'd been waiting for just such a moment "since birth," he told me over drinks one night. Even as a child, when he and his family sang his favorite Christmas carol, "Good King Wenceslas," "I wanted it to be better." If he were running the Choral Society, he could have "one thousand people sing 'Wenceslas' exactly as I think it should be sung." (He was counting the audience.)

Although John had a lot of experience conducting small and midsize groups in college, and had spent a year as the assistant conductor of the Harvard Glee Club, he'd never conducted a large group of adult volunteers and never a group in New York. It was a wonderful opportunity.

John went to the rector's office to speak with John Andrew, the priest-in-charge. The room was imposing in its elegance and grandeur, but John wasn't nervous. Like any good lawyer, he had all the points he wanted to make lined up in his mind. It was over in thirty seconds. He'd barely finished making his case before Father Andrew quickly answered, "Yes, yes, of course." There was nothing to decide. As the choir's assistant conductor he was next in line. He was also talented, hard working, and perhaps more to the point, he was willing to do this enormous job for free (at least initially). The position was his.

The first night John stepped up to the podium was toward the end of October, and it was pouring rain. John's new assistant conductor, Simon Yates, who had only gotten the call from John the week before, was caught without an umbrella. During the warmup a big drop of rainwater fell from Simon's head and splashed onto the keyboard. No one in the choir noticed, and the two men had a quiet laugh together. Then John raised his baton. This was our signal to get to our feet for the warm-up. John nodded to Simon. In one of the most wondrous buildings in New York City, roughly ninety adults were about to come to musical life under his command. It was the moment he had been waiting for since birth. What must he have been feeling? "In a word, panic."

Suddenly he was responsible for everything. "Can we do opera choruses next season?" "*Bohemian Rhapsody*?" "I'm allergic to perfume. Please tell the choir to not wear perfume or cologne." The first time he handed out seating assignments for the concert, a small crowd descended on him demanding changes. "But I'm always in the front row! My husband won't be able to see me back here." Every day, his e-mail box was flooded with people raising one issue or another. "Where can we put our purses so they won't get stolen while we sing?" "Can we wear black tops instead of white at the concert?" No problem seemed to be too small to bother him with. Once, a chorister found a half-full coffee cup at the end of rehearsal and, instead of throwing it away, handed it to John for disposal, much like a kindergartner would.

John was also now the sole contact between the Choral Society and the church, and he had to interact with the church regularly regarding scheduling of rehearsal spaces, the budget, and our repertoire.

The true source of John's panic, however, was a musical one. Mozart's father wrote that the performer "must spare no pains to discover and deliver correctly the passion that the composer has sought to express." But instead of spending the few hours we had each week shaping the music into the work of art the composer had intended, and fine-tuning the mood with carefully applied dynamics, we were learning notes. Between the people who didn't look at the pieces during the week, forgetting what they'd learned the Tuesday before, and those who missed rehearsals and never learned the music in the first place, we had to go over the same notes repeatedly. While John was going over them for the billionth time, those who felt they knew them—which may or may not have been true—would chat, chat, chat away, sometimes with the very people who needed to pay attention the most.

There were other distractions. Over the years, choir members had developed various methods for keeping the rhythm, like tapping their feet or patting their legs or bobbing their heads. John would look out over the erratic panoply of personal motion and try to corral the rhythm. It must have been like trying to mark time with a bunch of people with headphones in their ears.

There was never enough time to reach his musical goals, and every week he had a little bit less of it. The snack break halfway through rehearsal kept growing, along with an amount of time set aside at the end of the night for announcements: "I'm organizing a sing at a different church this Saturday and looking for volunteers" or "Please remember to vote this weekend."

There were issues in the soprano section. Not all the sopranos had the high notes. John would call out, "There's no shame in not singing if you don't have the note," but everyone would sing it anyway. It's a macho thing. Most sopranos would rather die than admit they don't have the high notes.

And there are never enough men, a common choir problem. Robert Shaw once joked about auditioning men. "There are always a few special rules for tenors," he said. "I ask them to make up a note and hum it—and if George [George Szell, the Music Director of the Cleveland Orchestra] can find it on the piano, they're in. . . . George says three tenors made it this year just by blowing their noses." Nationally, women outnumber men in choirs two to one (making the odds of my finding an eligible man pretty dismal). When Peter Julian e-mailed about joining the Choral Society, John wrote back inviting him to come to the next rehearsal. "He handed me the Bach *Magnificat* and the Vivaldi *Gloria* and told me where to stand. No audition, nothing. Just sing. My soprano friend was miffed that I didn't have to audition—she had had to audition—and I simply told her the rule: Tenors get in free!"

It's also difficult to recruit younger singers. According to some recent studies, more than two thirds of choir singers are over forty, and in one of the largest choral surveys ever conducted the median age was fifty-seven. At this rate it's just a matter of time before the entire Choral Society is in the grave.

There was one other big consideration. When John took over the choir we were a line item in the church's music office budget. The church got all the revenue from the ticket sales, but there were inklings that this arrangement was no longer working. At times John had to buy toilet paper because church officials let him know that it was going to be a while before the existing supply would be replenished. Shushing people for two hours while he spoon fed them notes and buying their toilet paper was not the dream he'd cherished since birth. Something had to be done.

I'D NEVER REALLY given much thought to running a choral society. You just tell people where to be and when, and what to sing, and there isn't much more to it, right? Don't drink or eat food in the church, wear black on the night of the concert, blah, blah, blah. What's the big deal? I took it all for granted and didn't really pay attention. For me, the choir provided an ever-so-brief intermission from my endless circuit of self-doubt, self-loathing, and fear, and I didn't really care about what went on behind the scenes. This was my escape. This was how I made my life better. I've tried other amusements: learning to kayak, playing the banjo, and dancing hip hop. But I came in dead last in the one and only kayak race I entered, I absolutely sucked at banjo, and I was so bad at hip hop that people in the class actually laughed at me. I'm just not good at most things. My greatest pleasure in life comes from two pursuits. The time-tripping other-world journey of researching and writing books—when I get to delve into an idea or event, or a person, and for a few dreamy, immersive years I have the enormous pleasure of figuring out how to bring to life whatever I've discovered. And singing. What makes singing special is that it's the one skill I've tried that makes my life better and it works even though I'm not particularly great at it.

But John saw the Choral Society not "as an escape, but rather a route to something finer." He was determined to transform us from a hobby choir to one that could take on the most challenging choral pieces ever written. He was going to hold us to a standard, and then "not allow us not to achieve it," as he later e-mailed me. "This was Brahms's own maxim with his women's chorus in Hamburg: *'Fix oder Nix'*—to the mark, or nothing." (Or, more crudely, fix or nix.)

John came up with a plan to bring the choir "up to code," and then he took it slowly. The first rules he instituted seemed so slight. Like "No tapping your feet." Or any other form of marking time. It was such a perfectly reasonable thing it barely registered. He went after the chatterers next. If people started talking during rehearsal, they were immediately stopped. John didn't yell or scream. He very simply and calmly informed us all that from now on, if he was rehearsing another section we were to sit quietly and listen. Years later, with the advent of clickety-clakety iPhones and other devices, he added a "no texting" clause. "This was all about changing without seeming to change," John explained. "It's about steadily and insistently improving without seeming to exert pressure or anxiety to do so."

The new rules kept coming. Music had to be learned before the rehearsal, not during, and every week he e-mailed us a list of pieces to have ready. He sent out score markings, with dynamics and note corrections, and we were expected to write them into our music in advance. The breaks that had reduced our actual weekly rehearsal time were eliminated. He also cut down the number of announcements at the end, and to make sure they were kept brief, he made them all himself and we were again instructed to sit quietly and listen. No more reaching for your coat or putting your things away. That invariably necessitated repeating some of what had been said, and from now on, not one second of rehearsal time would be wasted.

Or missed. People had always been casual about attendance.

The *American Idol* finale is on! But serious choirs have serious attendance policies. Leonard Bernstein was kicked out of the Harvard Glee Club for not showing up enough. Now, if you missed more than two Choral Society rehearsals you had to attend the make-up rehearsals John started holding a few times each semester. If you didn't attend a make-up rehearsal when needed, you were in danger of not singing at the concert. Or worse. Like Bernstein, you could lose your place in the choir.

Then John announced that everyone had to reaudition. *Oh, for the love of God.* I couldn't believe I had to endure that trauma *again*. John quickly explained that he wasn't going to kick anyone out, he just wanted to learn all our voices. But I didn't quite believe him. I also knew there was more to it for the soprano section. He needed to ferret out who *really* had the high notes.

The key to hitting high notes is getting your voice properly warmed up. To make sure my voice was ready for my audition, I ran through a series of vocal exercises as I walked to the church. Except I didn't want anyone to hear me so as soon as anyone got too close I clammed up. "La, la, la," stop. Act natural. Wait. Gone? "La, la, la," stop. I had to start and stop constantly, like some maniacal wind-up toy. I never got sufficiently warmed up. By the time I arrived I was in such a state of panic I said to John, "Could we just cut to the chase? You need to know who has the high notes. Let's get it over with." John was the last person I wanted to hear my voice, and in that moment I wished I could go back and sing for the strangers on the street. But apparently I'm getting okay at auditions. I reached the high notes.

While all this was going on, John was developing a recruiting system for building the choir. He started by asking everyone to rope in their friends. "Over the years," Choral Society tenor Roland Jarquio told me, "we've come to joke about the toaster that I'm due for signing up so many of my friends." John was also pretty well connected in the choral singing world, so he put out the word to all the collegiate choral conductors he'd worked with to send any graduating singers our way. He wanted the Choral Society to become *the* destination choir for New York–bound singers. Finally, he advertised our auditions on the Vocal Area Network (VAN), a website for vocal groups in and around New York. "There is ruthless competition among the different choral societies in town for great singers who are also dynamic volunteers and will be effective at bringing friends/family/coworkers in to hear the concerts. My aim is to put our chorus right up in the front rank during each annual audition cycle."

The efforts paid off. We got better, and over time our reputation grew. "We were sought after," said Milton Justice, a tenor who'd been singing with the choir since the 1990s. "I was often a greeter for auditions [people who volunteered to welcome those auditioning] and I could hear the auditions. Unbelievable the quality that we were getting for a volunteer choir. Many had music degrees and had come to New York to break into the music world. We were either the stopping-off place on the way to a career or we were the place they went once they took on other jobs. Whatever the reason, the choir was expanding and the quality of singer was improving."

Perhaps it was due in part to the fact that we were so welcoming. When soprano Lucia Rivieccio decided to join a choir, she auditioned with another well-known choral group first. It was very formal, she wrote. "I clutched my little Mozart aria, handed over my performance resume, sang my heart out, was asked to read some German cold, and that was it. While I was waiting outside the audition room, no one talked to me. There were current choir members there and they talked about the black tops that all the women were expected to order that year and the pearls and the fancy summer vocal programs in Ravello or Rome they had all just flown in from." But when she showed up for her audition at Grace Church, she was first taken to a parlorlike room. "While waiting my turn, I was offered tea and cookies, and Laddie [a bass in the choir] sat on one side of me while this fellow soprano Emily sat on the other. Both were so wonderful. . . . I could see immediately that this wasn't a choir of divas (although we do have our moments) or one-upmanship, these people really cared about each other, their conductor, and the group as a whole." We've always been a friendly group: Tim Bohn, who auditioned when Bruce was running the choir, told me that after he sang he stood waiting anxiously to hear if he'd made it or not. Bruce looked up from the piano and asked, "Do you like martinis?"

As time passed we attracted some of the best sopranos in the city, and the near-impossible-to-find men. Our ratio of women to men began to improve. While there are double the number of women in most choirs, in the Choral Society of Grace Church it's closer to three women to two men. We're also doing better in terms of age. More than half of our choir is in their thirties and younger, and 25 percent are in their twenties.

John made one more change that was so terrifying I practiced for hours every day to make sure I was ready for it. He knew it would be one of the more fearful changes he'd make, and he waited a few years after taking over the choir before introducing it in 2004. We were going to break up all the voice parts and sing in what is referred to as quartets. Before this, we always sang in sections. All the sopranos rehearsed and performed together, all the altos sang together, and so on. Now, instead of singing under the protection of a sea of fellow sopranos, I would have an alto, tenor, and bass around me.

"When John first told us that we were going to sing in quartets, my bottom jaw dropped," tenor Milton Justice told me. "Oh my God! What am I going to do without my security blanket! Unlike the new kids on the block, many of us from the old days were less than superior musicians." Barbara was nervous, too, it turned out. "It's the safety of the many," she e-mailed. "You tend to follow and you hear your part multiplied. When you sing in quartets, you have to know your part because if you don't, it's obvious to your neighbors. It's not safe at all."

The first time we did it my fear vanished. I loved it. Everyone did. "It's like going from two dimensions to three," said Roland Jarquio. "What is flat takes shape. And when the harmonies are just right, it's like you've created a hologram out of thin air. But it's ephemeral, so you have to keep infusing it with energy for it to stay alive."

The collaborative effort of keeping that hologram afloat gave me my first visceral understanding of harmony, an experience that later intensified when I sang soprano 2. "Physically," Roland observed, "the sensation is one of connection . . . [it's] a buzz. You make a contribution of sound waves and airwaves, and something more complex, something you couldn't possibly produce on your own, comes back to you. You constantly adjust your contribution. And it's focusing—or getting lost—in this feedback loop of producing sound and enjoying your labor at the same time. It requires more concentration than if you were producing sound or singing on your own, say, in the shower, and thus you really do get lost—in the sense that you can't worry about anything else in your life at that moment."

The bliss of getting lost was a theme the people who talked to me about singing in quartets returned to repeatedly. "Physically it feels like I disappear," Emma Berry said. "No, not disappear—I feel like there is a space above my head that we all meld into, that it is the purest form of together, a spiritual unworldly space." Soprano Christina Davis called it "a sort of structured and collective ecstasy."

"In a large choir like ours, it's easy to feel like one singer's contribution doesn't matter much or to lose a sense of co-operation with other voice parts," soprano Rosemary Demos told me. "Singing in quartets brings the music back to a feeling of intimacy and balance. I've loved being able to listen to individual voices singing right next to me on parts other than my own. It's both energizing and stabilizing to be surrounded by all four parts. And the musical harmony spreads itself into my overall sense of well-being. After all, there aren't too many chances in ordinary life to be in perfect cooperation with other people. Singing fulfills that need."

"In everyday life, it is easy to say you are listening when you are not," said soprano Elizabeth Abrams, who is a music teacher and the choral director at Grace Church School. "When you are singing in quartets, there is no faking—you must be listening." As Barbara put it, "The payoff is huge because when your voice blends with someone else's well, you've created something new and beautiful. It actually confirms why you sing in a choir. You don't do it because you love your voice; you do it because you want to blend with other voices to make harmonious sounds."

There was one more very large and important reward. "What I found to be happening once we began singing in quartets was that I became a much better musician," said Milton Justice. "When we were in sections I was often not aware that anyone but the tenors existed." Renata Morgenstern agreed: "It helps you to hear the piece sooner than if you're sitting in a sectional. And it made me learn the music faster than I might otherwise, because I feel an obligation to the men sitting on either side of me."

All the changes John introduced were having an effect. In time, people stopped tapping their feet (mostly), or talking during rehearsal (usually), and now they mark their scores and learn the music in advance (generally). I never miss rehearsals unless it's absolutely unavoidable, and I'm not alone. As Rosemary said, there aren't too many chances in ordinary life to feel like this, and most of us want to be here for every one of them.

One big issue remained in those first few years after John took over: we needed to become financially self-sustaining. John Maclay was the first director of the Choral Society who was not a member of the Grace Church staff, and the relationship between the Choral Society and Grace Church had already begun to change. We were still the Choral Society of Grace Church; neither side wanted to break up. "They give us a home and an identity," tenor David Beatty told me over lunch one day. "We fill the house three times a year." But the sides had come to an agreement. The Choral Society would no longer have a line item in the church's budget. As with every other outreach group at Grace, we were now responsible for covering our own costs.

After choir rehearsal, it was tradition to head over to the Cedar Tavern, a local bar and restaurant (now closed) that for many years had been a hangout for various well-known artists, writers, and musicians and, for a decade or two, the kick-back home for the Choral Society. "We sang from seven to nine thirty and drank from nine thirty to twelve," bass Tim Bohn said. "We spread out over many tables," Milton Justice remembers, "and were extremely popular with the waiters and waitresses because we tipped well. David Beatty had instigated a policy: a hamburger, two beers, twenty dollars a person. I'm sure many of us had perfect attendance because we wouldn't dare miss such a fantastic social event." Around those tables an informal board of advisers was forming, and in addition to socializing and flirting, sometimes until 3 a.m., issues about the choir were raised, discussed, and resolved. John had started out as a member of the choir and everyone wanted to make sure that he and the Choral Society did well. "When I was gossiping in the back with the basses during rehearsal," Tim Bohn said, "John was one of the people I was gossiping with."

One night after rehearsal, talk at Cedar Tavern once again turned to the future of the Choral Society. "We knew we had to take charge of our destiny," said David Beatty. Their chief concern: what was the best way to raise money? At that time any donations for the choir were funneled through the church. Alto Miriam Alimonos pointed out that not everyone who might want to help the choir would feel comfortable with making a check out to a religious institution. The decision was made to become a 501(c)(3) so that we could solicit tax-deductible and church-free donations. Tenor and lawyer Peter

Julian had experience in this area, and he volunteered to set it up. A Certificate of Incorporation was filed in 2003, and soon after, a sponsorship program was put in place. Miriam would sometimes stay up after midnight stuffing envelopes with requests for contributions and, later, thank-you cards.

Milton compared the board of directors' early days to a start-up company. "None of us had ever done it before and it was raw and exciting. I loved the fights, and the crazy ideas that never saw the light of day, like singing at a Yankees game." They'd argue about ticket prices, the wording on signs outside the church, and the program, but in the end it was all about the music.

The start-up they formed is now a successful, established business. After only one year of operation, John and a couple of members of the board met with the priest-in-charge of Grace Church and the church's CFO. It was decided, John told me, that "we had demonstrated enough operational responsibility to be able to run the entire budget (tickets, contributions, dues, plus all expenditures) for the next year and beyond." It was also decided that the Choral Society would begin making payments to Grace Church for the use of the space.

The board had done its job well, and while many choirs struggle financially, we have always had enough to pay for anything from the relatively inexpensive *Mass in Straitened Times* to orchestra-heavy pieces such as Beethoven's *Missa Solemnis*. A little more than 35 percent of our revenue comes from the sponsorship program, grants, and benefits, 15 percent from the dues ($100 per choir member per season). But the largest chunk of all—nearly 50 percent—comes from ticket sales. We have only three performances a year, two during the holidays and one in the spring. There were many reasons for limiting the number of performances, sheer exhaustion, for example. It was also important to reduce the number of times people had to sell tickets. I've been singing with the choir for close to thirty years, and my friends and family have bought a lot of concert tickets in that time. But that meant the revenue from a mere three performances had to bear a large portion of the financial weight for an entire year. Of the three, the highest hopes were always on the holiday concerts. Those are the moneymakers, and this has always been the case. In a nineteenth-century book about the music scene in New York, the author mentioned that the principal income for the Oratorio Society of New York (which is still in operation) came from annual December performances of none other than the immortal, dependable Handel's *Messiah*. "For most choral groups," John e-mailed me, "you'll find those holiday season spectaculars are extremely important. With two Christmas concerts comprising a little over two-thirds of our ticket revenue, we store up funds so we can take on a more ambitious project in the spring."

Bottom line: we really need to fill those holiday seats. But according to the Vocal Area Network website, while we're rehearsing every Tuesday night, so are thirty-nine other choirs, and over two hundred more the rest of the week. With two hundred–plus choirs potentially putting on holiday concerts, all around the same time and all needing the money every bit as much as we do, how do we fill *our* seats?

Meanwhile, I had my own financial concerns. My credit-card balance was climbing up to the thousands due to veterinary bills for my cats, I couldn't make my next health-insurance payment, and estimates for my dental work were now up to $12,000, none of which would be covered by insurance. Haydn had said of his most financially straitened times that he was nonetheless so happy that "when I sat at my old, worm-eaten clavier, I envied no king his great fortune." Easy for Haydn to say. He had the corresponding satisfaction of having written music that is referred to by some as being among the highest achievements in Western music.

WHEN REHEARSALS BEGAN that winter, I started hearing about something called the Virtual Choir. It was created by Eric Whitacre, a forty-one-year-old conductor and composer whose "Lux Aurumque" was on our program that year along with the Haydn. It wasn't until a few months later that I got the full story, from an online video of Whitacre giving a TED talk.

TED (Technology Entertainment, Design) is a nonprofit "devoted to ideas worth spreading," where invited speakers are given an eighteen-minute forum to present those ideas. Whitacre was explaining how the concept of the Virtual Choir had come to him in 2009, when a friend sent him a link to a high

school girl singing the soprano part from one of his compositions. The girl's face flashed on the large screen behind him.
"Hi, Mr. Eric Whitacre," she begins, so sweetly it's almost
painful. "Um, my name is Britlin Losee and this is a video I'd
like to make for you. Ever since I heard your song "Sleep" I
have been addicted to music. Music is my life, it is my heart,
it is everything," she gushes, "and, um, you've touched me."
There's a long pause before she starts to sing. You almost
think she's going to lose her nerve. Then, as the camera reveals
a piano in the background, with a stuffed bunny and a teddy
bear on top, she gazes reverently and shyly upward and sings
with a voice so sweet and pure that Whitacre was reduced to
two words—"My God." For a few seconds his mind was reeling. Then he had an idea.

Whitacre began by writing a request on his blog for singers
around the world to buy a specific recording of "Sleep" and
to upload videos of themselves singing along. When edited
together the result was so promising that he decided to try
something else. He posted a video of himself conducting "Lux
Aurumque" and once again invited singers to upload videos
of themselves singing. This time he asked them to follow his
conducting instead of a recording. One hundred eighty-five
singers from twelve countries responded.

In the small section of the "Lux Aurumque" video he played
for the audience at TED, Whitacre's looks rival most movie
stars'. He's dressed in a simple black T-shirt, and he's moving his hands up and down caressingly, almost seductively.

Like all good conductors, he's mesmerizing. The faces of the singers slowly appear and swirl across the screen. Each one of them is every bit as engaging as the young Britlin Losee, and from their collected voices emerges a shimmering, incandescent harmony with the same otherworld quality you hear in the expansion of the universe, when astronomy professor Mark Whittle translated the notes from the historical record to the standard octave of today, and for the first time the universe's haunting chorus was heard.

In Whitacre's chords, the suspension and the resolution are present at the same time, and "it feels," Whitacre described in another interview, "like you're standing still and moving at the speed of light at the same time." Everything that was present shortly after the moment of creation is in those chords. This is how the universe sings. The audience at TED leapt to its feet. At my computer, my heart was racing.

The video of Whitacre's TED talk went viral. If singing is about community and bringing people together, the Virtual Choir had just taken it to a whole new level. Harnessing the power of the Internet, the Virtual Choir instantly flew around to the world's computers, grabbing up hearts at speeds and in numbers that were inconceivable as little as six years ago. Even the massive Lincoln Center *Messiah* sing couldn't top this in terms of size and reach. At the beginning of his talk, Whitacre had confided, "I wanted to be a rock star." He'd already made a name for himself in the choral world, attracting throngs of admirers and choral groupies wherever he went, but in those eighteen minutes, he'd crossed over to a whole other level of fame. "It was one of the highlights of my life," Whitacre told me later during a telephone interview. "I was standing on that stage and I've never in my life felt this experience where the audience had its own intelligence. There's this buzz, this kind of hum, this electricity of curiosity. I've never felt it before." I could feel the snap of that current months later, sitting alone at my desk.

Over thirty years ago the composer Randall Thompson wrote, "The truth is that while many a serious composer has been working in seclusion—doubtless producing fine works—a whole new medium of expression has come into being: nobody ever before had such a medium of communication as composers have today in the amateur chorus. . . . Boys and girls, men and women all across the country and around the world are ready and waiting, eager for new music to perform, fully as eager for it as an Esterhazy prince ever was to have a new quartet!" But it wasn't always so easy to reach them. Now, with a keystroke, singers can find their works and each other, and composers and conductors can summon choirs out of thin, electric air.

At the end of his presentation, Whitacre premiered the Virtual Choir 2, singing "Sleep." This time he received over two thousand videos from fifty-eight countries. Soon after, I learned that plans for a Virtual Choir 3 were in the works. I wanted to do it. Then I thought it through. The best thing about choir is that your voice is one of many. To participate in the Virtual Choir, you have to upload a video of yourself singing your part, alone and exposed, every imperfection out there for all the world to see. I imagined a video of myself up on YouTube. What if *that* went viral?

I went to Eric Whitacre's website. There was a page for the next Virtual Choir, and a place to sign up to receive information about when it was happening and how to participate. I wasn't going to do it, I told myself. Then I put myself on the mailing list. And waited.

Ave Maria

Written by Franz Xaver Biebl in 1964

**Performed by the Choral Society of Grace Church
most recently in the Winter, 2005**

The audience at the Metropolitan Museum had to wait a few minutes while 136 of us entered the Medieval Sculpture Hall and lined up around the Christmas tree. Later we'd learn that our collected exhalations had raised the humidity to destructive levels for the centuries-old tapestries that hung around the room. I never saw them. I remember walking into the hall behind the fifty-two-foot-tall choir screen, hammered into existence by Spanish ironworkers in the eighteenth century, but at first everywhere I looked I only saw a blur of stone-cold gray. I was vaguely aware of statues ringing the room, and tombs and various depictions of the dying Christ, but the tapestries didn't register. It was too dark and I was too excited to focus. John caught alto Mary Horenkamp's eye as she walked past, and she looked "as excited as a little kid getting in line for Space Mountain at Disney World."

Everything brightened up when we came out from behind the screen. The angels floating among the branches of the Christmas tree were lit from underneath like ballerinas on stage in a Degas painting, adding to the opening-night-like thrill. We were all packed in tight, the choir, the audience, and a small brass ensemble; I was a few rows back, nestled beside the sparkling lights from the tree. I tried not to fidget while the rest of the singers lined up behind me. I looked down at the famous Neapolitan Baroque crèche just inches away and immediately flashed back to the elaborate train sets of my brother's youth, the tiny re-creations of various scenes, little trees, little people, the more detail the better. John barely noticed the crèche or the tree. He was too busy trying to commandeer eye contact from the groups of overly excited singers arrayed on either side of it. I couldn't believe I was there. I'd been coming to the Metropolitan Museum every December for years to see that tree, and now here I was, about to sing a piece that was written over four hundred years ago, in a room full of statues that may once have vibrated from monks singing the very same words I was about to sing now: Kyrie eleison. "Lord have mercy," the words at the beginning of almost every musical setting of the ordinary mass. *Remember to think, remember to look at John, remember to sound good.*

This was the concert where a music critic for the *New York Sun* wrote of us, "I have been concentrating on religious music this month and so have heard several large singing ensembles, but none has been even close to the level of professionalism of this strictly volunteer group. . . . The choir expertly combines the two most important tools in a singer's armamentarium: discipline and passion. They are amateurs in the best of all possible senses."

THE FIRST CHRISTMAS concert at the Metropolitan Museum was in 1955 and featured the Vienna Boys' Choir. Since then the Met has hosted 145 Christmas concerts, 132 of which have been in this hall. Early-music groups including The Waverly Consort, The Aulos Ensemble, and Pomerium Musices have all performed here many times, but the group that has sung at the museum the most is an all-male a cappella choir from San Francisco called Chanticleer. They took their places in the hall for the first time in 1991 and they've been singing there every year since. When we sang at the Met we concluded our concert with a piece that I'm sure Chanticleer has sung every time they've performed here. It's their signature piece—the haunting and ethereal "Ave Maria," by the German composer Franz Xaver Biebl.

Choirs love to sing it and audiences love to hear it, but sometimes when people compliment this piece they do it with a sightly dismissive air. It's nice enough, they'll say, but it doesn't deserve a place alongside Bach or Handel or Palestrina. It's true that the "Ave Maria" is not a work of complex beauty, but there's a reason it's so popular.

In 1964 Biebl was fifty-eight years old and the director of the Bavarian State Radio Broadcasting Company's Department of Choral Music, which he founded. A fireman from his local church summoned up the nerve to approach him and ask him to compose a piece for his fire company to sing at an upcoming singing competition. Like eisteddfods in Wales, singing competitions were a very big deal in Germany at the time. People lived and breathed singing, and winning these competitions was an honor and a matter of local pride. Everyone got into the act. Factory owners and police departments would rally around their employees' choirs, sponsoring them and cheering them on. Years later Biebl would admit to his friend, music scholar and choral conductor Rev. Dr. H. Wilbur Skeels, "I am just a little composer of little songs. There is only one Beethoven, only one Mozart, but there are many people who speak music. Therefore we must find our niche, find what we do best, and do it while we can." Biebl knew his niche. Mozart and Beethoven composed for the greatest singers of their time. Biebl sometimes wrote for firemen. But he wanted his firemen to win.

Part of Biebl's challenge was to give the firemen a song that didn't require the skills of an Enrico Caruso to produce music so painfully sweet that after they sang it the judges would tell everyone else they might as well go home, because they had a winner. Biebl came back to the firemen with "Ave Maria." The text is from the Angelus, a practice of devotion to honor Mary and the Incarnation of Christ. It's a simple piece. Anyone who can sing can manage it. Yet something about this arrangement of notes goes straight from the heart to the voice, and anyone listening today can immediately recognize the audio essence of love.

At first, though, response was muted. No one, not even Biebl's daughters, remembers if the firemen won, and the song didn't get a lot of repeat performances. The first people to go mad about it were Americans, which was ironic because the first time Americans were introduced to Biebl, they threw him in prison.

According to Reverend Skeels, Biebl had been a reluctant draftee during WWII, and in 1944 he was captured by the Americans while a patient in a German field hospital in Italy: "He woke up to find an American GI guarding the ward, and a bowl of fruit (which had not been there before) on his bedside table. An American officer walked in and the GI greeted him very familiarly (something like 'Hey, Capt'n!') without springing to attention and saluting (as would have been the case with German soldiers). At that point, said Biebl, he felt he understood for the first time the real meaning of American democracy and he was glad to have become a non combatant!"

Biebl was taken to Fort Custer in Michigan (there were hundreds of prisoner-of-war camps located in the United States) and immediately put in charge of a choir. "The Americans secured copies of American folk music for him, which he began arranging, to mix in with German songs he had to transcribe from memory—although I think he may have had some access to local library holdings with the camp's permission," Skeels writes. Life at Fort Custer wasn't hard, and the American soldiers were generous and fair, and as a result Biebl had a soft spot for Americans ever since. Later, as the director of choral music at the Bavarian State Radio Broadcasting Company, he would take every opportunity to invite American choirs to come to Germany to sing.

Conductor Thomas Sokol accepted his offer, and on January 28, 1970, he arrived in Germany with the Cornell Glee Club. Biebl was so taken with their singing he gave Sokol copies of some of his music and asked if he would consider including one or more of them in their repertory. "Ave Maria" was Sokol's first choice. They started performing it soon after they returned to the states, and it wasn't long before collegiate ensembles at Harvard, Amherst, Michigan, and many others were introducing "the Biebl" to their audiences. Once Chanticleer recorded it in 1990 it became a bona fide hit. "Now, several decades after Sokol brought the piece to the United States," writes Michael Slon, in *Songs from the Hill: A History of the Cornell University Glee Club,* "few choristers in America have not sung—or at least heard—this beautiful music."

In 2005, four years after Franz Biebl died, the Choral Society of Grace Church stood around a twenty-foot-tall blue spruce at the Metropolitan Museum bursting with barely containable excitement and singing his little song. If there had been a competition, we would have won. It took a lot of work, however, to perfect that unassuming little song.

"SOMEONE IS SINGING this note," John sang at our first rehearsal of the holiday season. "Someone is still singing this note"—he continued to sing as he walked around the room, trying to figure out who it was—"when they should be singing this." Then he switched to the right note. More than one hundred people were singing four different parts at once. How could he hear one single person singing one single wrong note? I immediately started singing very, very quietly. Then it hit me. It was going to take me months and all my musical resources to learn my one part. John already knew them all. We were doing fifteen pieces for that performance. That meant that John had come to rehearsal that night having already learned eighty-five voice parts, and that wasn't count-ing the orchestra, which he also had to know.

In the months leading up to the beginning of our season, while I'd been watching TV or playing on the Internet, John had been poring over piles of scores, making notes, and be-coming so familiar with eighty-five-plus parts that he could detect a single wrong note. "I have many voices in my head," John once said during rehearsal. Learning every part, however many, is just one item on one of his many to-do lists (all of which are maintained in Excel). "Miracles don't just happen," choral conductor Robert Shaw said, "they're earned." And a lot of miracle-earning takes place behind the scenes.

It begins with selecting the music. There are six centuries of compositions to choose from, and the first sign of a good conductor is how well he knows the field. John is unequivocal about his first criterion. "We need to pick the best of the best. Life is too short, unfortunately." The music has to be challenging, but not too challenging. "I remember begging John to sing the Mozart *Mass in C Minor*," tenor Roland Jarquio told me, "and him saying he didn't think we were good enough. We've since sung it twice." Also, as much as we might love the *Messiah* or *Elijah,* there should be a mix of periods and styles and music from different countries. John also has to take into account the time of year. "You are singing a program during the season of Christmas (Advent, really), in a major metropolitan church. Is the Verdi *Requiem* really going to be appropriate for that?"

Once the music is selected he will spend months studying the scores. There are practical reasons. For example, he has to know where the hard parts are and where cues may be necessary. But more important, while I'm focused on my one part, he has to understand the piece as a whole. This is when John spreads many parts around him and really gets to work. Before he walks into the first rehearsal the entire performance must be in his head, like an internal iPod.

"The more we can detect about what a composer wanted and expected to hear," writes Jameson Marvin, emeritus director of choral activities, senior lecturer on music, Harvard University, and one of John Maclay's mentors, "the closer we will come to the true meaning of the music."

Having that audio image in his head is one thing; bringing the choir to the same musical understanding is another.

We have to hear what he hears. For the next fourteen weeks, 152 people of varying musical tastes, skills, and abilities will gather at Grace Church—152 people who are thinking about bills, work, TV, or who they have a crush on. If they're thinking about the music at all, most likely it's about their part only. Somehow John has to corral all those disparate needs and get everyone to think not only about his or her part but everyone else's part and what the orchestra will be doing at the same time. He has to transform 152 soloists into a choir.

Every week, as we sing our way down his rehearsal to-do list, John is constantly matching up our sound against the concert in his head. There is a swirl of things that must be attended to: rhythm, balance, tuning, and phrasing, and the most important aspect of these components, *ensemble* rhythm, balance, tuning, and phrasing. "Quieter!" he called out one night. "Let the basses shine through!" There was a particularly moving bass line, but none of the other parts knew because we were drowning them out. Of all the musical elements we'll have to work out as we learn this piece, ensemble rhythm is perhaps the trickiest to communicate, hear, and achieve. Rhythm has an emotional life, and it has to be felt by all of us in unison. Adhering too strictly to tempo, for instance, can elicit a mechanical performance. The timing needs a certain elasticity, it needs to breath. Sometimes you want to hold on to a note a little longer or let go a little sooner. Ultimately, it has to come from John, but it also comes from listening to everyone around you. You have to find the perfect midpoint between following John's pulse and blending with the other voices in the choir.

John can be quite poetic about what he wants. Once, when an alto asked about a cutoff right before the sopranos come in, he brought his palms together and answered, "I would overlap slightly, like you're holding the orchid which you're handing over to them." Tuning (finding the right notes) was going to be particularly crucial for this mostly a cappella concert at the Metropolitan Museum. There'd be no place to hide. "You have to land on the chord like a gymnast sticking her landing," John said. Finally, attention to phrasing is important in order to make musical sense. There is a rise and fall of feeling throughout every musical line. For instance, if you knew you were going to follow the words "I love you" with "Will you marry me," that would change how you said "I love you." Each note has to be imbued with the understanding of what comes next, of where we're going with it all, and the piece as a whole, or it loses meaning.

While all this is going on, John will periodically remind us of the orchestra that will eventually join us. Sometimes it's to reassure us. "Don't worry, there will be violins underneath you playing your part." Sometimes it's a warning. "Now is the time to panic, because the orchestra is going to drop out at this point and you're on your own."

The best times are when he gives us some fact or piece of history about the music that brings to life a time that previously seemed too far away to feel real. When we were working on the *Lord Nelson* Mass, the piece Haydn wrote after his benefactor had fired most of the wind section, John explained how in some sections Haydn had substituted our voices for those missing instruments. "You're there doing what a clarinet or oboe would have been doing." Then he talked about the war, and how Haydn had to borrow musicians from the military band for the premiere. The better the stories, the more expressive our singing.

While John prepares us musically, there is also a more prosaic side to arranging for a concert. For our last performance, John's concert to-do list had sixty-four items on it, such as, "rent 15 stands and 15 lights with power strips" and "distribute paychecks and collect W-9s" (from the orchestra). Between John, the board, and a small group of volunteers, someone has to make sure that everyone has the right music, dues are collected, people are keeping up with attendance, donors are found, programs are printed, announcements are sent to the press, and so on. But it is John alone who on top of spending hours perfecting the standing charts for concerts ("place cards" for separating clashing voices and surrounding less confident singers with more confident ones) processes the online ticket orders and puts the tickets in the mail. He accomplishes all this while holding down a high-level corporate law job with a ringside seat to the financial crises of the last few years.

Week after week, year after year, as he works his way through his multiple and extensive lists, making hundreds of decisions, it's no surprise that every once in a while he makes a questionable one. The year after we sang at the Metropolitan Museum we were invited back. It was great news, but there was a catch. Due to the effect on the tapestries, they were forced to reduce the number of singers in the hall. Only half of us could return. It shouldn't have been a problem; although it was a shame we couldn't all participate, the gig paid very well and the Choral Society needed the money. It was also a relationship we wanted to cultivate. "I think we all secretly believed that it could lead to something more spectacular," board member Milton Justice said. "*Elijah* at the Temple of Dendur perhaps." It was to become the biggest crisis the choir has ever faced.

Over the summer John sent out an e-mail letting us know that we'd be returning to the Metropolitan to sing. After explaining why it had to be a much smaller group, he asked us to recommend who we thought should participate. I asked to be included, but when he wrote back saying, "Sorry, no," I wasn't surprised. Half of us had to be disappointed and as one of the so-so singers I was already prepared to be in the disappointed half. Still, it was a musical death. The choir was going to go right on singing in that fabulous place beside that magical tree without me, as if I were never there or had never been so excited I could barely stand still. It was an awful glimpse of that inevitable time to come, when I will have taken my last breath, never to raise my voice again. The choir will reshuffle and immediately fill in the empty space I've left and go on, no one remembering the soprano who once stood there.

At our first rehearsal in the fall John repeated the announcement. After that we didn't hear anything for a long time. The silence created mystery, and everyone kept wondering, "What is going on with the Met concert?" Week after week we expected more announcements. Not everyone had asked John directly if they could sing, so many people were wondering, who would be singing? Were there going to be auditions? Since John wasn't saying, we asked each other. "Are you singing?" "Do you know who is?"

John had decided to keep references to the gig at a minimum. "There is nothing more demoralizing," John explained, "than being in a choir and having endless chatter about what the 'elite group' is up to." It was a reasonable decision. No need to rub everyone's faces in it. "More communication would lead to more conflict," another board member said. The lack of it, however, led to strife.

"We're grown-ups," alto Dimitra Kessenides said to me. "We put our trust in you [John], why don't you come out and tell us how it's going to be?" Others felt the idea of excluding anyone was just wrong. "That's not what choir is about." All or none. Emma Berry, an alto originally from the United Kingdom, explained that in England there is never a formal audition, and pretty much anyone who shows up is welcome. "Community choirs bring people together for a social activity that happens to be singing," she told me.

At every rehearsal, the whispering continued, and it began to undermine the common goal we'd normally be focused on.

"It shook up my respect for him," one person told me. John had more than achieved his goal of taking the choir from an escape to "a route to something finer," but that made it all the more painful when it was taken away.

Even though I had quickly gotten over my own disappointment, it made me realize that I ask an awful lot of the choir. It has to make up for everything bad, and that year had been particularly horrible, in ways both large and small. The wars we were waging were getting to me. Once, I tried to get an accurate count of how many soldiers and civilians had died to date and I had to give up. The numbers were elusive, hinting that the true totals were too horrible to be allowed to circulate. *What's that apocalyptic chorus we do, the one with the pains of hell and the bottomless pit? Yeah, let's do that one.* All that sadness and death that I felt powerless to prevent, but that year it was one tiny death that destroyed me.

Not long before choir started, a sick bat made its way into my apartment. Of course he made his way into *my* apartment. I'm like an animal-in-distress magnet. The bat was so small the wildlife organization I contacted thought he might be a lost baby, which made me all the more frantic to help him. Animal Care and Control said they'd send a truck, but they didn't know when and I was afraid my cats might hurt him. I looked online and found a biologist in Texas who explained how to catch him. Let him land, she said. He'll go to sleep within minutes, and then you can easily slip him into a box. The bat picked a spot in the curtains. I waited, then climbed up on my desk, shaking and crying the whole time. He was a bat, after all, and I was scared. But I managed to get him into a box and safe from cat harm. When the Animal Care and Control guy arrived we took the bat downstairs and tried to release him. For a few brief seconds it looked like all would be well. The bat flew straight up into the air like a beautiful, spooky butterfly. I was about to cheer his freedom when he fell to the ground, flopping. I stood and watched him struggle. *Please get up.* "We'll have to test it for rabies," the guy told me. Which meant they were going to kill him. I considered rescuing him from the Animal Care and Control worker, but then what? I did nothing when the man put him back in the box and drove away.

A couple of weeks later rehearsals resumed. Over the course of the semester my sadness for the little bat faded, as did the bad feelings that had arisen among the choir. "When you sing, you cannot be sad for long," a chorister was quoted as saying in a British study of singing, and that seemed to be both my experience and that of the choir overall. There is a lot of science to support the universality of this response. Almost every study of singing I've read comes to the same conclusions: singing feels great and it's good for you. It decreases feelings of anxiety, loneliness, and depression. Singing also makes you smarter. Children who sing in choirs get better grades, according to a 2009 study by Chorus America. Choristers are also nicer. They were found to volunteer significantly more than the general public and to give more money to charity.

There are physical benefits to singing, as well. Studies show that brain activity involved with learning music helps counteract the effects of aging and cognitive decline. In her book *The Secret Life of the Grown-Up Brain,* Barbara Strauch includes joining a choir as one of the things you can do to enhance neuroplasticity. Music increases gray matter and the number and strength of neural connections in the brain. My 100 percent score in the cognitive abilities test in her book may be attributable to a lifetime of continually learning new (and really hard) music. When archaeology professor Steven Mithen, a nonsinger, took singing lessons, it changed his brain after only one year.

Singing relieves tension headaches and symptoms of irritable bowel syndrome. It helps people with asthma and bronchitis to breathe. It's "particularly useful," according to the authors of the paper "The Therapeutic Effects of Singing in Neurological Disorders," in ameliorating the effects of a variety of neurological disorders, including stuttering, Broca's aphasia, Parkinson's disease, and autism. Singing also reduces stress, which can aid in healing and can improve the immune response. People who listen to music before surgery are more relaxed and need less anesthesia, and afterward they get by with smaller amounts of pain medication. Music can calm our hearts or makes them race, lower our blood pressure or raise it. One study indicated that making music together actually reduced stress more than sitting back with a magazine or newspaper. Even singing about death is good for you.

Researchers discovered that a choir singing Mozart's *Requiem* showed an increase in s-IgA, an immunoglobulin that enhances our immune defense.

Everywhere I look I find confirmation that music is having a positive physical effect. It excites all the areas of the brain that have to do with emotion and emotional memory. It brings atrophied limbs back to life. People who can't remember information for more than a few seconds at a time can sing a long, complicated piece of music. Stroke victims who can barely speak can sing. People who can't talk at all can still sing. After being shot in the brain, Congresswoman Gabrielle Giffords learned to talk again by singing. Finally, when all other memories are gone, victims of Alzheimer's are still able to sing songs from their long-distant youth. Music is the last thing to go.

Musical vibrations move through us, altering our physiological landscape, leaving us in better shape than when they found us. There are so many positive effects it's not surprising that there are so many singers. The Chorus America study found 270,000 choruses. And they're not just in churches, but in schools and on concert stages large and small all across the country. According to Chorus America, 32.5 million adults sing in choirs, and the figure goes up to 42.6 million Americans when you include children. That's up from the 23.5 million in their 2003 study.

None of this is a revelation to anyone who sings. Are you feeling bad? Join a choir. Lonely? Join a choir. Sick? Join a choir. One senior quoted in a paper about singing and senior citizens said, "I have a degenerative condition and my health is slowly getting worse but it is the one thing I can do at the same standard that I was doing before so it gives me a sense of reality and something that I can always do." The results of singing hold true no matter who you are or even whether you can really sing. In the 2005 paper "Effects of Group Singing and Performance for Marginalized and Middle-Class Singers," investigators found that "the emotional effects of participation in group singing are similar regardless of training or socioeconomic status," and that "group singing and performance can produce satisfying and therapeutic sensations even when the sound produced by the vocal instrument is of mediocre quality." The quotes from the homeless schizophrenics in their study could be coming from people in my choral society. "When I sing," one of them said, "it's almost like a high. . . . I have something to look forward to every week— the music."

There may soon be an explanation for why even singing sad music feels good. There is a hormone called prolactin that has a tranquilizing and consoling effect. It's released in tears of sorrow and while women nurse their infants. Ohio State music professor David Huron is preparing to test his theory that prolactin is released when we listen to music that is sad. He believes this is why sad music makes us feel better and why we seek it out even when we're not sad. Although Huron will be looking at the effects of listening, not singing, since singing in a choir also involves listening, presumably whatever he finds would apply to choristers as well.

By the time of our regular holiday concert at Grace Church, people had forgotten their disappointment about the Metropolitan concert and their anger over the way it was handled. The pleasure of singing had prevailed. If Huron and others are right, how could it not? Music could be the perfect drug. All benefits and no unpleasant side effects.

In the end, the episode had humanized John. So he wasn't perfect. We weren't all beside that spectacular tree in that wonderful hall, but on the night of our own holiday performance we had our miracle nonetheless. There's a moment that happens sometimes, when we stop after singing *forte*. For a few brief seconds our last notes continue to reverberate around and above us, like cheers dying away. It's just an echo, really, but it feels as if the church and the universe want to hold on to the sound we made as long as possible. Sometimes John even looks up afterward, like there's something or someone to see up there. When this happens we all stand as still as we can, holding our breath, as if a single inhalation might break the spell. Even the audience freezes. You won't hear a single program rustle or a cough. "I don't understand how we don't crumple over," bass Tim Bohn told me, "and I have to fight to maintain my bearing." That night it happened, and the music did what it's supposed to do. Everything we felt, good and bad, was swept up and turned into beautiful unison, something I've never been able to achieve any other way. "*Lasset das*

Zagen, verbannet die Klage," we sang. Abandon fear, banish lament.

Every choir season brings out a thousand acts of compassion and understanding, many of which we never get to see. "When I joined the chorus," choir member Sabina Brukner told me, "I was morbidly obese, close to five hundred pounds. John always placed me at the end of the row during performances so that I could sit down if I needed to. As I lost weight, he slowly moved me into the center of the chorus. This was never discussed; I never asked him for this consideration. To this date, I consider this to be one of the greatest subtle acts of kindness anyone ever showed for me when I was that heavy."

A few years after the second Metropolitan concert, on John's tenth anniversary, members of the choir wrote tributes, which were printed in the concert program. "In the dead of rehearsal you sometimes resemble a mad professor, attempting to perform some dangerous kind of musical alchemy. And every season . . . you manage to make something from nothing. It takes a lot of work (from all of us) but especially from you." "Tuesday is my favorite day," people stated repeatedly. "For those of us who have hitched our wagon to your star for the past ten years," one person wrote, "it has been the journey of a lifetime. You do all the work and we just show up." "You've made me a better singer."

At least two people left the choir over the Metropolitan Museum debacle and we have never sung there again. "But to this day," Milton Justice said, "whenever I go there and I walk

through the portals into the space where we sang and say to
whomever I'm with—*I sang here*—there is always a look of
awe. It was truly a beautiful experience. . . . Singing amidst
the History of Civilization gave us that sense of being a part
of an art form that was a tradition that went back through
all times. You were suddenly part of that tradition that had
shaped mankind. It was pretty remarkable."

LAST WEEK JOHN sent us an e-mail to prepare for
the first rehearsal for our spring concert. Once again, while
the rest of us took a month off, John had studied, marked,
scanned, and uploaded over 120 pages of music to a website
he had created, where in addition to those scores we would
find links to articles about the music, recommended recordings, and an online site with audio files for all our parts so
we could practice. For all of that he was only able to mark off
two items from his rehearsal to-do list. The following week
he lugged five heavy bags of Ralph Vaughan Williams scores
to Grace Church.

Alto Emma Berry told us about how she had shown up early
for rehearsal in the gym one night and found John setting
up the chairs, as he does every Tuesday night. One hundred
fifty-two singers means 152 seats. "Do you want some help?"
Emma offered. He welcomed her assistance, but because this
was John the chairs had to be arranged just so. He set up three
chairs and then spent minutes adjusting them, moving each
a fraction of an inch in one direction or another. "We've set

up a hundred and twenty-five chairs, there's roughly twenty more to go and he's constantly adjusting three." She stood and watched him. Shuffle, shuffle, shuffle. Pause. Examine. Shuffle, shuffle, shuffle. She pantomimed him moving each chair a fraction of an inch and then changing all three again. After watching him for a couple of minutes she couldn't take it anymore. "If you move that chair again I'm going to slap you." John ignored her. He was going to get them just right.

Recitative
The Chatham Street Chapel Riot

On Friday morning, July 4, 1834, a mostly black congregation gathered in the Chatham Street Chapel in downtown New York to celebrate Emancipation Day, the day in 1827 when slavery was outlawed in New York. The exercises were opened with a prayer, then three choirs, one white and two black, rose to sing the first five verses of a hymn written especially for the occasion by the Quaker poet and staunch abolitionist John Greenleaf Whittier. After a reading of the Declaration of Independence, Lewis Tappan, a prominent abolitionist, stood up to speak. The chapel had originally been constructed as a theater, so when Tappan stepped up to the pulpit he was actually standing on a stage. This was surrounded by an orchestra pit, where the choirs were situated, house seats, and finally the galleries, which rose above and circled the floor. Soon after Tappan began speaking, "a

distant roar was heard in the streets like the shout of an assail-
ing army." Within minutes a mob appeared and swarmed the
galleries. They were mostly quiet at first. But when the next
speaker took the stage the mob had found its voice, and whenever he tried to speak they drowned him out with screaming
and cursing. From then on, according to one newspaper account, the only time they were silent was when the choir sang.

Mayor Cornelius W. Lawrence, who had been in office for
only a few months, was said to have been present, along with a
group of watchmen. Watchmen were roughly equivalent to today's police patrolmen, but without the professional training.
This particular group of watchmen stood by and did nothing.
In one newspaper account, one of the watchmen would later
justify their inaction, describing the mob as "the most civil
fellows for rioters he ever saw," which was mostly true. No one
was seriously injured. Of course, had a large group of black
men similarly invaded a white service, yelling and cursing,
their civil heads would have rolled.

The mob was becoming increasingly threatening, and the
chapel's sexton suggested that the congregation pack it in and
try again on another day. The committee organizing the service asked about the following Monday evening, July 7, but
Mondays were reserved for the rehearsals of the very prominent and all-white New-York Sacred Music Society. Founded
in 1823, the Sacred Music Society was a choral society that
had by this time "become the most powerful, prosperous, and
public-spirited musical force in the city," according to author

Vera Brodsky Lawrence in an account of the nineteenth-century New York music scene. The conductor, Ureli Corelli Hill, would go on to become first president and conductor of the New York Philharmonic Society. The sexton approached Oliver Lownds, the president of the Sacred Music Society, and asked for permission for another group to have the space that night. According to Lewis Tappan, Lownds had responded cheerfully. "At this season of the year," Lownds said, "but few attend and we can use the lecture room," a smaller room in the chapel. The committee, in turn, paid fifteen dollars for the use of the main hall.

Temperatures soared in the days leading up to July 7, and people were dying due to the heat. But "the spirit of man was a volcano in comparison of the weather," wrote one witness of the events to come. Once again the mostly black congregation gathered in the Chatham Street Chapel. Unfortunately, word about the temporary arrangement had not reached all the members of the New-York Sacred Music Society, and not long after the service began, a group of choristers arrived for their regular Monday-evening choir rehearsal. From here, newspaper accounts of what happened next diverge, depending on the paper's stand on abolition. *The New York Sun* published the most sober and spare account. "Another riot occurred at the Chapel in Chatham Street night before last, between the blacks and whites. The disturbance originated in consequence of a misunderstanding in relation to the right of the New-York Sacred Music Society to occupy the building that evening.

After some few blows a body of watchmen entered the Chapel, and turned both blacks and whites out of doors, and locked the gates. The president on the Sacred Music Society (Mr. Lownds) was not present."

It was an important point to make. For Lownds, being present at the scene of this particular riot would have been complicated for two reasons. In his day job, Lownds was what was called a police justice (a judge). The police department, courts, and prisons were not as clearly separated in 1834 as they are now, and the police justice also oversaw the watchmen. Had Lownds been a member of a group that had taken part in a riot, it likely would have been one conflict of interest too many. Second, the police justice was an elected position and Lownds wouldn't have wanted to alienate anyone on either side of the abolition issue.

The vice president of the Sacred Music Society, who had not been in contact with Lownds, walked past the congregation and the choirs and climbed the steps to the pulpit. According to antiabolitionist accounts, he approached the speaker and "in the mildest manner, stated the facts" and asked them all to leave. Presumably it would have also been explained to him in an equally mild manner that their use of the hall had been cleared with Lownds and paid for, and that another room had been made available to the Society for their rehearsal.

In some accounts the members of the Society had initially accepted this explanation and left quietly. But a mob had once again gathered outside and they convinced the choral society to go back inside and take the chapel. Attempts were made to drag the speaker, Benjamin F. Hughes, the principal of African Free School No. 3, from the stage, blows were struck, a collection box was broken, benches were thrown, lamps smashed, all amounting to $25 worth of damage, or about $550 today. People were severely hurt according to one newspaper account, and no "dangerous wounds" were reported in another. One newspaper proclaimed without a shred of irony that the New-York Sacred Music Society were the rightful owners of the space that night, having paid $850 in yearly rent "for the purpose of practicing and improving themselves in sacred harmony." Only two months before, in the very same chapel, close to two hundred members of the New-York Sacred Music Society had gathered to perform Handel's *Messiah,* where they would have joyfully sung about the "prince of peace."

The only people arrested that night were four black men. One of them, Samuel R. Ward, a former slave who was only sixteen at the time, wrote his side of the story in an autobiography that was published in 1855. (Ward doesn't name the official he describes below, but he was probably referring to Dr. William Rockwell, the vice president of the Sacred Music Society, who was also a health commissioner.)

That meeting was dispersed by a mob led by a person holding a lucrative political office in the city. This gentleman . . .
thought to do as he pleased with the blacks, kicking them about

at will; and while Mr. Hughes was speaking, ordered other parties to come in and occupy the building. Seeing resistance made by some of the coloured people, and fearing he might receive a blow for a kick, he elevated a chair over his head, and stood witnessing the mêlée [that he] himself had begun, when Mr. Jinnings knocked him over with a well-aimed missile. Leaving his men to fight or run, as might seem wisest, this general of the mob escaped from a window 22 feet from the ground . . . [becoming] the only man injured in the affray.

The blacks were victors; every white man was driven from the place. But while a few of us lingered, a reinforcement of the white belligerents came, and, finding some few lads of us in the place, they drove us out with a rush to the door. Then they commenced beating us in the most cowardly manner. The public watchman arrested the parties beaten instead of those committing the assault, and it was my lot to be among the former number. For the crime of being publicly assaulted by several white persons, I was locked up in the watchhouse throughout the night.

The four young men were brought before the police magistrate the following morning, and one of the arresting watchmen made a brief statement. "Thur was a row in Chatham Chapel last night, and these niggers was there." Instead of being released when no one appeared to bring charges against them, as other prisoners were, the four were remanded to Bridewell, a prison that had been in use since 1775 and was in such ruinous shape that it would be torn down a few years later. At Bridewell the men were thrown into a filthy cell with nineteen others, including murderers. "When the prison cup was offered us to drink from, and when the prison food was brought us, feeling our innocence and our dignity . . . we refused both." They were discharged when Ward's father arrived the next day to pay their bail.

The imprisonment roused Ward to action. "My oath of allegiance to the anti-slavery cause was taken in that cell on the 7th of July, 1834," he wrote. He immediately began educating himself, and three years after his imprisonment he was delivering an oration before the Literary Society, where he was a member. "It was my first public attempt at public speaking," and Lewis Tappan, who was at the church the night of the riots, was proudly present. From then on, Ward traveled the country speaking against slavery, often accompanied by Frederick Douglass. William Henry Seward, the governor of New York and Abraham Lincoln's future Secretary of State would say that he'd "never heard true eloquence until I heard Samuel R. Ward speak."

In 1849, a year after the New-York Sacred Music Society had given its last concert, Ward founded a newspaper called *Impartial Citizen.* It was "designed to aid in the elevation of the Free Colored People, and to support and urge the doctrines of a Righteous Civil Government." He retired to Jamaica in 1855, where he worked as a minister and a farmer until his death in 1866.

The Chatham Street Chapel was demolished in 1836.
What follows are the final stanzas of the hymn composed by
John Greenleaf Whittier for the July 4, 1834, Chatham Street
Chapel service. It was sung to the tune of an air called "Old
Hundred."

And grant, Oh, Father! that the time
Of Earth's deliverance may be near,
When every land and tongue and clime
The message of Thy love shall hear—

When, smitten as with fire from Heaven,
The captive's chain shall sink in dust,
And to his fettered soul be given
The glorious freedom of the just.

Missa Simile est Regnum Coelorum

Published by Tomás Luis de Victoria in 1576

Performed by the Choral Society of Grace Church
in the Winter, 2008

Four centuries ago a music teacher in Rome took his new mass to a small group of young and very tired seminary students and asked them to sing. The school was the Collegio Germanico, and it had been founded in 1552, in response to Rome's anxiety about the decline of Catholicism in Germany. The idea was to educate young Germans and send them home as clergy. The fact that they'd soon share the responsibility of revitalizing Catholicism for an entire country must have weighed on the seminarians. But their teacher had taken the prayers they said every day and set them to music so enchanting, I believe it would not only have infused them with the certainty that they were up to the challenge, but more than any book or lecture, it would have reinforced the conviction that it was a glorious burden to bear. Perhaps like Brahms and his choral society of women three hundred years later, the music so enraptured and reinvigorated them that when night fell they didn't want to stop singing.

If the evening was warm the students would have continued on at La Pariola, a lush and fragrant vineyard that had just been donated to the college by the pope as a much needed place to rest. It had also quickly become a favorite place to sing. By the time they reached the final movement, any remaining languor would have vanished completely. Their teacher had saved the best for last. Every note of the unassuming Agnus Dei II is so quiet, unhurried, and subtly affecting that one minute they were a bunch of overworked college students, and the next minute they were thrilling to chords so heavenly it must have felt as though the vineyard was packed with angels. If the Agnus Dei elevates a nonbeliever like me, I can only imagine the Heaven they soared to.

"You felt it, didn't you?" they may have asked each other afterward, wanting to revel in this shared, special knowledge. Something this astonishing doesn't come out of nowhere. It must mean something. Surely the feeling working its way through them, bonding their hearts, perhaps forever, was nothing less than the grace of God.

The composer was Tomás Luis de Victoria, a former student who'd returned to the *collegio* as a teacher a few years before. At twenty-eight years old, Victoria wasn't much older than the seminarians, none of whom were under twenty. He must have been as exhilarated as his students were when they sang his new mass. Until that day, the music he'd written had been only in his head. Now it was floating all around him. The vineyard where they loved to sing was the entrance to catacombs that bore the name of Saint Hermes, who was said to cure the mentally ill and whose name was given to the ball of electric fire now more commonly known as Saint Elmo's Fire. Singing these shimmering prayers at the mouth of that final resting place would have charged them with a deep sense of the eternal. The idea that a single soul lay beneath the ground would have been unthinkable—the dead had to be someplace where this entrancing music was reaching them, too. God would have felt so close that it wouldn't have been such a stretch for them to believe that maybe He could hear them as well.

THERE WASN'T A lot of music at the Collegio Germanico in the beginning according to Father Thomas D. Culley, S.J. (Society of Jesus), in his book *Jesuits and Music*. Ignatius Loyola, who formed the Jesuit order in 1534, had restricted the use of music. *"Jesuita non cantat,"* the saying goes. Jesuits do not sing. While Loyola lived, students weren't allowed to sing the Divine Office (the daily prayers) or have instruments in their rooms. But Loyola died in 1556, and by 1571, when Victoria returned, Loyola's limits had largely disappeared. Two years later Rector Michael Lauretano was put in charge. A former choir boy, Father Lauretano never lost his love of singing, and he immediately instituted a formal program of music.

There wasn't a lot of money when the *collegio* was first founded, and to help defray costs, the institute accepted students from England, Spain, and Italy who paid to be there and were called the *convittori* (convictors; in this case student boarders). Victoria, who hailed from Spain, had been a *convittore*.

In 1573 Pope Gregory XIII gave the college a generous endowment and the following year the Palazzo di Sant' Apollinare for its new home. No longer cash-strapped, the leaders of the college made the decision to separate the students. The *convittori* would remain at the old school and the German seminarians would conduct their studies at Sant' Apollinare. To help ease the transition, a parting ceremony was planned. Years later one of those students would gratefully describe how Victoria had set Psalm 136 (he used the Septuagint, or LXX, Bible) "to the melodies of a sorrowful lamentation," in order to "solemnize the complaint at the most bitter parting." Psalm 136 begins: *Super flúmina Babylónis, illic sédimus et flévimus.* "By the waters of Babylon we sat down and wept." But if you listen to it now you have to strain to hear a note of sadness. Had I not known this piece was written to acknowledge a difficult passage in life, I would have guessed it was written to celebrate the commencement of one of the most joyous. There's a sense of exultation in every measure, sometimes subdued, sometimes bursting forth, as if Victoria couldn't contain himself.

In 1575, the year before Victoria published the *Missa Simile est Regnum Coelorum,* the pope issued a bull decreeing which feasts would be celebrated with singing. It was clear that Father

Lauretano's musical efforts at the college had the pope's full and complete support. According to Joseph F. MacDonnell, S.J., "The students would sing the entire office on 52 feasts as well as the daily celebration of Mass. In addition, occasional motets were sung about 200 times a year and all students received daily instruction in music." They were even directed to use a half hour of their free time after dinner to practice.

There was so much singing, it's amazing the seminarians got any schoolwork done. A former German student from the pre-Lauretano days could barely believe his ears when he visited. He described Lauretano as "not so much Rector as some sort of master of ceremonies," and urged that "the excessive singing . . . be diminished." Germans were "too given to singing" as it was, he reminded them, and their studies were being "greatly hindered by that insatiable and perpetual custom of singing." But he was too late. By then the college had become known throughout Europe for its music and the formerly nonsinging Jesuits were now singing all the time.

Four centuries later, the *Missa Simile est Regnum Coelorum* still holds up. Regardless of my lack of faith, I am not immune to the glory this music excites, and I'm convinced that when I sing the Agnus Dei II I'm experiencing the same feelings those religious students did all those years ago. The only difference between what I feel and what the German seminarians felt is how we interpret those feelings. For that small group of students, the music would have connected them to God. For me, it connects me to them.

• • •

IN HIS PAPER "The Plural Pleasures of Music," Ohio State music professor David Huron writes, "Music could not have achieved or sustained such prominence without tapping into the biology of pleasure," and aesthetic philosophers have "underestimated the complexity, richness, pervasiveness, and importance of neurological pleasure." I may have very different beliefs from those of the seminarians, but we all have (had) a body and something happens to it when we sing.

To clarify just what that is, I went back to Daniel Levitin's book *This Is Your Brain on Music.* I was looking for studies that focused on the physiological components of two aspects of singing that I believe the seminarians and I would have experienced in common: that singing in harmony feels good, and that singing with other people is invigorating. While I didn't find an explanation of the physiology of singing in harmony, there was something in his book that gave me an idea for experiments scientists could try that might. Levitin writes about how pitch is literally mirrored in the brain, that "the brain represents it directly. . . . We could place electrodes in the brain and be able to determine what pitches were being played to a person just by looking at the brain activity." That would mean that when we sing in harmony, the neurons in our brains are likewise literally, not figuratively, firing in harmony. Our brains are directly representing that harmonic interval, humming together in perfect neural rapport. So experiments that were done with one person singing could be repeated with two. First measure the brain activity of one person singing. Then bring in another person and continue to measure that person's brain activity while the second person joins the first in harmony. What else happens? Do other areas of the brain that perhaps didn't come to life when one person was singing, come alive when there are two? Or maybe the same areas of the brain are involved, but more intensely? What is different about the brain activity of someone singing alone versus someone singing with others?

A 1992 experiment with macaque monkeys and the discovery of cells now known as mirror neurons might one day help explain the intensely social pleasure of harmony. The experiment revealed a group of neurons that fired in both the frontal lobe of the animal performing an action and the frontal lobe of the animal watching. In short: the observing monkey's brain mirrored that of the active monkey. Evidence has since been found that seems to indicate that humans have mirror neurons, too. At a TED talk in 2009, neuroscientist Vilayanur Ramachandran told the crowd, "It's as though this neuron is adopting the other person's point of view. It's almost as if we're performing a virtual reality simulation of the other person's actions."

We're not only mirroring *what* we see someone doing, but *why* (Rizzolatti, 2005). When we watch someone having their dinner for instance, we're not just observing their actions, but also inferring their intent and possibly their feelings (i.e., to satisfy hunger or taste food they enjoy). "Mirror neurons make emotions contagious," psychologist Daniel Goleman explains, "letting the feelings we witness flow through us, helping us get in sync and follow what is going on." Empathy may be, among other things, neurological. We are hardwired to try to understand how another person feels. If empathy is hardwired via the mirror neuron system, some scientists propose, people with autism may have impaired mirror neuron systems, and that singing, which activates "brain regions that largely overlap with the human mirror neuron system [MNS] may improve their ability to interact."

Could a better understanding of the mirror neuron system illuminate something of what happens and what we feel when we harmonize? When we harmonize we must constantly check our tuning against what everyone else is singing and also must match their rhythm. Researchers have found that just as the observing monkey's brain mimicked the active monkey's actions, singing engages the motor network of both the singer and the listener. We hear the music and our premotor cortex responds (the premotor cortex is a part of the brain involved in the perception and preparation of movement). So sound, and not just observation, is playing a part in activating mirror neurons. Music engages a number of areas of the brain, such as the superior temporal gyrus, which is used to process sound and also emotion. In Katie Overy and Istvan Molnar-Szakacs's study comparing music makers and their audience, "Being Together in Time: Musical Experience and the Mirror Neuron System," the researchers have taken these discoveries and put forth a hypothesis they call the "Shared Affective Motion Experience" model, or SAME. The SAME model proposes that given the neural networks involved in the brains of both the musicians and the audience, by synchronizing our experience (of sound, movement, and emotion), music conveys a sense of "being together in time" with other people. This perception is so powerful that it occurs even when someone is listening to music alone.

Their SAME theory may also explain in part how a choir is able to maintain ensemble rhythm. Mastering the skill of being rhythmically flexible is hard enough. A choir must learn how to accomplish this *as one*. Conductor Jameson Marvin uses several interesting techniques to train choral singers to feel a group rhythm, some of which seem tailor-made to test the authors' hypothesis. "Teaching a choir to sing with good rhythm means to sensitize choral singers to a unanimous group pulse. Their internal clocks must be taught to perceive sound by the same scale of measure." Marvin's exercises all involve, strangely enough, silence. "Energy can fill silence, energy can be felt," Marvin explains, and "energy that is harnessed together, in silence" can help people feel the same rhythm. In his simplest exercise, everyone in the choir counts to seventeen. First the conductor establishes the tempo by giving the choir a straightforward four-beat pulse: 1-2-3-4, 1-2-3-4. The choir is then instructed to clap together on the first beat, count silently to themselves to sixteen, and then to clap together again on the seventeenth beat. "I will guarantee," Marvin writes, "that the clap on beat seventeen will begin occurring on beat fourteen, fifteen, or sixteen. It sounds like applause."

Clapping together on the seventeenth beat takes practice. In this exercise, ensemble rhythm is being learned without sound or movement but instead in silent perception of group sound and movement. Perhaps this noiseless rhythmic-empathy is achieved by the action of mirror neurons. Similarly, when we sing, rests (moments of silence) are bursting with energetic activity, with excitement, emotion, and anticipation. If you could scan the brains of one hundred people as everyone is simultaneously engaged in the beat, you might see one hundred mirror neuron systems firing like mad. The energy people feel might be the effect of all those mirror neuron systems in overdrive.

There are experiments that seem to confirm that shared rhythm does, in fact, contribute to shared feeling. A 2010 study found connections between music, emotion, and tempo. "The human mirror neuron system follows tempo changes and communicates that to the emotion center," according to Ed Large, one of the researchers. When we listen to music there's an emotional response in the brain that's based "at least in part, on the perception of movement" and, specifically, creative deviations in that movement, or tempo. No one enjoys a precise, mechanical performance. Rhythm needs to have an emotional life. Writer Justin Davidson describes this necessary manipulation of tempo in a *New Yorker* article about conducting. "In classical music," he writes, "time behaves like a Slinky, stretching and compressing without ever losing its shape." When this happens, researchers found that brain activity "that is consistent with the mirror neuron system" engages, and emotion and reward circuitry activations increase in the brain. We feel good.

It turns out that the nearly impossible and intricate fugues my choir sometimes sings are nothing next to the complex symphony of empathic neurological responses that take place inside our brains while we're doing it. Neurons fire to represent the pitches we are singing; the pitches we are hearing; the movements we make to hit each note; the movements we perceive others making; our feelings about what we are singing; and finally what we perceive about the feelings of our fellow singers. It's an intimate and precisely timed orchestration of shared neurological activity and it occurs whether we're singing the bawdy *Carmina Burana* or we're in seminary school singing our teacher's new mass.

If people do in fact possess a mirror neuron system, when we sing we're in a constantly expanding mirror neuron feedback loop. It begins with the conductor, who is mirrored by the choir, who are mirroring one another and are in turn mirrored by the audience. Everyone is simultaneously re-creating what everyone else is hearing and feeling (or trying to). Some composers often warn against trying to determine what they are trying to express. Ralph Vaughan Williams writes, "I feel very angry with certain critics who will have it that my 4th

Symphony 'means' war, and my 5th 'means' peace—and so on. If people get help in appreciating music from this descent from the general to the particular, good luck to them." But it could be that we can't help ourselves, that our brains are built to try.

Regarding harmony, one study indicated that harmonization activated the section of the brain referred to as Brodmann's area 38, which is one of the parts of the brain that is effected earliest by Alzheimer's disease. Maybe singing in harmony will one day be shown to mitigate some of Alzheimer's destructive impact. But the study of the pleasure of harmony has not yet captured the scientific imagination with any zeal, though it is perhaps the most crucial element of group singing. The difference between unison singing and the expansion into harmony is the same as the difference between love and the absence of love. You don't disappear within the group (or person) when you've found harmony (or love), you become more present and reverberatingly alive. One group of scientists became aware of the importance of harmony while investigating the role of singing in the lives of a large male-only choir in a remote area in Northeast Iceland. They began to notice how much the men preferred singing in harmony to singing in unison (Faulkner, Davidson, 2006). When not singing next to a same-voice singer, "none of them avoided listening to the other voices in a 'fingers in ears, singing in harmony' sense, rather the men seek an appropriate self to a 'different voice' balance. . . ." Once achieved, the men wanted to feel it again and again. "I fell for it straight away," one said, describing the feeling of being pulled along in "this sound, the harmony that you land inside of."

After listening to the men slam unison singing for more than ten years—it was a long term study—the authors realized that the men's "criticism is founded on the intrinsic quality of vocal and social interaction that singing in harmony facilitates and that singing in unison clearly does not." But they struggled to explain it. They recognized that when you're singing in a choir you're both an individual voice and part of a vocal team and that the group effort felt vital. "Through some kind of team personification, a collective becomes super-person, an extension and yet integral part of oneself." Or, put more simply, "There appears to be a heightened or at least different sense of self in this collaborative behaviour." But while they offered theories of "flow" experiences, and the possibility that harmonizing fulfills "a longing for more instinctive, non-verbal ways of being and interacting," it's clear that we have a long way to go in understanding what is happening. Whatever the explanations might be, "I would like to find it even more," a man in their study told them, "to find the sound with another voice. . . . You feel much better in harmony with others. Then you get that kick."

That kick is precisely the other avenue of research I wanted to explore. No one comes out of choir rehearsal more tired than they went in. "Every week when I go to rehearsal," my choral friend Barbara said, "I'm dead tired and don't think I'll make it until nine thirty. But then something magic happens and I revive. I wonder, how is this possible when I feel so wasted from the workday. And yet it happens almost every time." Just how *did* those seminarians sing as much as they did and still get all their schoolwork done? In the paper "The Perceived Benefits of Singing," authors Stephen Clift and Granville Hancox present the results of two choral-society surveys; 74 percent of the respondents said that singing made them feel more energetic, 76 percent said they felt "more awake and alert," and in one of the more interesting responses, 63 percent reported "tingling feelings in my body." These effects seem pretty universal. The studies I read were strewn with quotes confirming the enlivening effects of singing: "When I sing with them it's almost like a high." "I love it, I absolutely come home totally wound up and wired and love it, love it." "This is how I felt about the concert: ecstatic, elated, excited, joyful, grateful." "Usually we sing at night, I'm so high because of having singing, I'm on a trip. It's a drug for me, it's a real drug. . . ." Is there a physiological response in the body to explain these feelings?

A lot of papers state that the neurotransmitter dopamine is released in the brain when we sing. Dopamine is associated with feelings of pleasure and alertness, and it's released when we eat our favorite foods, have sex, or indulge in drugs such as cocaine. However, none of the papers I read cited experiments that substantiated this claim about singing. The closest I came at first was in Daniel Levitin's book *This Is Your Brain on Music*. "Dopamine is released by the nucleus accumbens," he writes. Levitin and his fellow researcher, neuroscientist Vinod Menon, studied fMRI (functional magnetic resonance imaging) brains scans of people listening to music, and "We found exactly what we had hoped." The nucleus accumbens was involved, along with all the areas of the brain they'd needed to see activated in order to say that listening to music does seem to be "mediated by increasing dopamine levels in the nucleus accumbens, and by the cerebellum's contribution to regulating emotion through its connections to the frontal lobe and the limbic system."

A more recent study by five Canadian scientists has shown the most direct connection to date. People were asked to pick their favorite music and indicate the parts of the music that consistently gave them chills. Then, using PET (positron emission tomography) scanning combined with a drug used to determine dopamine density, fMRIs, and measurements of the nervous system such as the heart rate and respiration rate, the researchers found a direct correlation between listening to music and the rewarding rush of dopamine. They also discovered another dopamine surge in the seconds leading up to a peak section of the music, in a different area of the brain, the caudate (which has been shown to be associated with the perception of beauty and feelings of romantic love). It seems that just anticipating the best parts is chemically rewarding. "Our results provide, to the best of our knowledge, the first direct evidence that the intense pleasure experienced when listening to music is associated with dopamine activity in the mesolimbic reward system, including both dorsal and ventral striatum." This may explain in part why people sing no matter how terrible their circumstances. Physiologically speaking, singing is one of the ultimate mood regulators.

That said, University of Connecticut psychology professor John D. Salamone says that dopamine has more to do with motivation than with pleasure, less to do with reward than with the benefits of sustaining a task, and that low levels of dopamine may also be related to fatigue. So the increase in dopamine levels from music may be responsible for getting us through rehearsals of demanding pieces like Beethoven's *Missa Solemnis* when we're tired, the energizing effects felt throughout and afterwards.

When I asked Stephen Clift, one of the authors of "The Perceived Benefits of Singing," why he thought singing was so invigorating, he offered these additional explanations. "I think this is probably a function of three or four factors: (a) singing is a physical activity and requires expenditure of energy, (b) singing requires concentration and focused attention and so is cognitively arousing, especially when singing in parts and needing to follow a score, (c) the nature of what is being sung is also important—music which is upbeat and high in tempo is intrinsically 'energetic,' and finally (d) if the singing involves performance, there is the inevitable factor of 'performance anxiety' (of a good kind—eustress rather than stress) and the wish to do well. [Eustress refers to positive stress, i.e., the kind you feel when you're excited about something you're looking forward to.] All of these factors combined means that singing together is going to be invigorating."

A day later Clift e-mailed me again, adding a fifth factor, the "social facilitation" effect. "It has been known for over 150 years that when people do things together they tend to perform more effectively and more quickly than when they undertake the same task alone—especially if it is skilled and well-rehearsed."

A 2003 study found significant increases in oxytocin in people who just had singing lessons. Oxytocin is a chemical that is sometimes referred to as the "love hormone" and, according to Daniel Levitin, enhances feelings of trust and bonding and is also released during group singing. "Early humans didn't sit and listen to music by themselves—music formed an inseparable part of community life."

Once again, it's not just singing, but singing with other people.

My search for scientific explanations for the positive results of singing also regrettably turned up three musical afflictions that fill me with dread: auditory hallucinations, tinnitus, and brain worms (also sometimes called ear worms). At one time or another I've briefly experienced each of them, and since then I've done my best not to think about them. I now know that any one of them could return and never leave.

It happened to composer Robert Schumann, who appears to have suffered from all three. One day he started hearing music in his head. At first it was wonderful, but soon after, he had trouble getting it to stop. From Clara Schumann's February 13, 1854, diary entry: "His auditory disturbances had escalated to such a degree that he heard entire pieces from beginning to end, as if played by a full orchestra, and the sound would remain on the final chord until Robert directed his thoughts to another composition." The problem quickly grew much worse. "My poor Robert suffers frightfully!" Clara wrote. "All noises sound as music to him. . . . He said many times that if it did not stop he would lose his mind."

Something similar happened to me when I was in my late twenties and at the lowest point I've ever been in my life. I felt trapped in a job and a relationship that were both making me desperately unhappy, and instead of dealing with any of it I was drinking. Out of the blue, random noise started occasionally resolving itself into music. Air conditioners, for instance, sounded like brass bands, and wind in the trees sounded like choirs. It didn't frighten me while it was happening, but since I knew I was hearing music that wasn't there, I was concerned that one day it might become more alarming. I was also distressed that something that had always given me such joy might turn on me. Fortunately, when I stopped drinking and addressed the reasons I had come to such a low point, the invisible marching bands went away. Schumann wasn't so lucky. From Clara's diary on February 17: "In the night, not long after we had gone to bed, Robert got up and wrote down a melody which, he said, the angels had sung to him. . . . When morning came, the angels transformed themselves into devils and sang horrible music, telling him he was a sinner and that they were going to cast him into hell. He became hysterical, screaming in agony that they were pouncing on him. . . . The two doctors who came only just managed to control him."

Fate wasn't through torturing Robert Schumann. He also suffered from what may have been a particularly unendurable case of tinnitus. Tinnitus is usually experienced as a ringing in the ears, but it can manifest in all sorts of ways: buzzing, whooshing, or even screaming. According to the CDC, 50 million people in America have tinnitus to some degree, 16 million to the point where they need to seek medical attention, and for 2 million of them it's so bad it affects their quality of life. In his book *Musicophilia,* Oliver Sacks describes how the music in Schumann's head eventually degenerated "into a single, 'terrible' note, an A, which played ceaseless day and night, with unbearable intensity." After that Schumann was placed in an asylum, which he never left. When I came to that part I threw down the Sacks book. I have a mild case of tinnitus. It's maddening, but as soon as I'm distracted it goes away. Given that tinnitus is incurable, the idea of one note playing nonstop forever is too horrible to contemplate.

Both Daniel Levitin and Oliver Sacks discuss another annoying, sometimes distressing audio anomaly called brain worms. These are the bits of songs that become stuck in your head on what feels like eternal repeat. I get them when I practice a little too much, but I can also get a brain worm from just the thought of the Beyonce song "Single Ladies," which I love. "Our best explanation is that the neural circuits representing a song get stuck in 'playback mode,'" Levitin writes, adding that musicians get them more than nonmusicians, and that OCD medications can sometimes minimize the effects. Oliver Sacks tells the story of one of the postencephalitic Parkinson's patients he originally wrote about in his book *Awakenings*. These were people who remained in trancelike states for decades before being awakened for a time by the drug levodopa, often called L-dopa. One patient who had a brain worm the entire time she was in this trancelike state said it was like being stuck in a "musical paddock" for forty-three years. They "tend to lie in wait," Sacks wrote, confirming my worst fear. Sacks's own earliest brain worm goes back more than sixty years, and like my Beyonce song, he can activate it by just thinking about it. Terrific. That means "Single Ladies" could torment me until the day I die.

I also found a discomfiting answer to an audio question I've had for some time. Whenever someone near me sings completely out of tune and doesn't stop, I think, "Can't they hear themselves??" We all go out of tune, but you hear it and adjust. Sometimes it's hard to tell if it's you or someone else, and the only way to be sure is to stop singing and listen. Some people, however, just go right on singing, apparently oblivious. Well, according to Robert Jourdain in *Music, the Brain, and Ecstasy*, if those people are over forty, two terrible things are happening that might explain why they seem so unaware. By age forty, Jourdain writes, "the ear is only a tenth as sensitive at its highest frequencies." *Wait, is he talking about the soprano notes?* A "high-frequency sound," he continues, "must be ten times more intense for it to seem as loud" as it did when you were twenty. "By the age of eighty, the decline amounts to the difference in volume between a whisper and a jackhammer." It gets worse. At forty your ability to detect pitch begins to go, and when you get to your sixties, "discrimination at all frequencies is only about a third to a quarter as good as formerly." As time goes on a B doesn't sound very different from a C. When I wondered if those people singing out of tune behind me could hear themselves, the answer was: maybe not.

Happily, our former associate conductor Dylan Chan, now a fifth-year resident in otolaryngology—head and neck surgery— at Stanford University, who plans to join a research laboratory studying the physiology of hearing and deafness, e-mailed me that while Jourdain's comments were true up to a point, there was no need for me to panic, and certainly not about the soprano notes. First, he addressed the issue of volume. "It is true that all of us lose hearing with age, and that this hearing loss starts at high frequencies and slowly progresses downward. At age 40, however, most people do not have significant hearing loss in the range relevant to singing; a high A is at around 880 Hz, which is well below the 2,000–4,000 Hz frequencies, that start to go first with age. By the time you hit 60, the lower frequencies begin to be affected, but again, the effects are fairly mild. Saying that the ear is 'only a tenth as sensitive' sounds bad, but is really not that bad; hearing thresholds are logarithmic, such that the difference between 40 dB and

60 dB—quiet conversation vs. regular conversation—is 10-fold. But people are well-known to have a very hard time distinguishing absolute hearing levels in the absence of comparison, so if you have a bit of a hearing loss, say, 20 dB, which would make your ear 'one-tenth as sensitive,' you may not even notice it out of context. The statement about the age of 80 being the difference between a jackhammer and a whisper is also misrepresented. Only a fraction of 80-year-olds have the kind of significant hearing loss in the singing range that would make this true."

Then he dealt with the issue of pitch. "While it is true that frequency discrimination can deteriorate with age, I'm not sure [about] the degree to which this occurs. Our discrimination is quite good to begin with, and tuning is so much more than discrimination at a single pitch—it has to do with matching a whole bunch of different overtones and involves a lot more high-level processing than what is going on at the level of the ear. Anyway, while it's true that some people have a hard time tuning, I don't think you can blame all of it on aging changes in the inner ear!"

Perhaps the strangest hearing "problem" I came across was in the reports of people who had near-death experiences that included music. I don't believe in life after death, but it's nice to think that the last thing I might hear is a song.

In 2006 the neuroscientist Jason D. Warren wrote, "The biological basis of musical experience remains largely unknown." But now we know a little more. There is no evidence to suggest that music differentiates between the bodies of those who believe and those who don't. I wonder: If the Canadian researchers could go back and scan the brains of those sixteenth-century seminary students while they sang, would they find shots of dopamine coursing through the same regions, rewarding their efforts in the same way it does mine? If Clift and Hancox could question them, surely the seminarians would report feeling energized, and a tingling sensation, which might be explained by the dopamine or the oxytocin or both.

The seminarians would have taken these wonderful feelings as confirmation of the righteousness of their beliefs. Because for Victoria and his students, singing was about lifting up and exciting the soul. That's part of the reason I sing, too, but the seminarians took it more literally. They were solemnly and earnestly sending up a musical prayer to celebrate the glory of God. Music meant solely for pleasure was, in fact, frowned on by the Catholic Church. But I don't sing solely for pleasure, either. I don't know anyone who does. Everyone I know gets something more from it, regardless of what they believe.

Even the Church recognized that beauty and pleasure have their place. When the bishops met at the Council of Trent, in the sixteenth century, their decrees addressing sacred music seem mostly concerned with keeping the text clear and perceptible, so that it "may reach the ears of the hearers and quietly penetrate their hearts." So while they insist that "the entire manner of singing in musical modes should be calculated not to afford vain delight to the ear, but so that the words may be comprehensible to all," they go on to say, "and thus may the hearts of the listeners be caught up into the desire for celestial harmonies and contemplation of the joys of the blessed." I believe their point is that as long as the music was in support of the text, which remained intelligible, a gratifying harmony was not only acceptable but an effective means to open hearts and inspire devotion.

Composing a beautiful and inspiring mass was therefore a job requirement, and Tomás Luis de Victoria was more than up to the challenge. On top of all his skills and talents as a composer, he was a recently ordained priest. He would have approached the task of writing the Mass with all the reverence the bishops could have hoped. But before Victoria had become a teacher, composer, and priest, he'd been a singer. When Father Lauretano, his superior, wanted singing added to the sacred ceremonies, "in order to stimulate, by a certain pleasure, the soul, urging [it] to a desire of that which is celebrated in song," Victoria would have known in every atom of his being what kind of music would stimulate souls (and singers). The very restrictions laid down by the Council of Trent aided him. Their emphasis on the careful attention to text, combined with a concession to beauty, brought forth the measured and slowly evolving harmonies of the *Simile est Regnum Coelorum*. It gives singers all the time in the world to revel in just how good those harmonies feel, particularly in the Agnus Dei section at the end.

Here's what happens when you sing it. The Agnus Dei is an eight-in-four canon. Two choirs of four different voice parts sing through the prayer using a simple method of call and response. The first choir sings a section of the text and then the second choir comes in, repeating the same musical line. They keep doing this until they've made their way through each section of the text and four canons are going at once. (Rounds such as "Row, Row, Row Your Boat," are the simplest version of canons.) As the voices pass each other by in prayer, in an unhurried tempo, harmonies that are inexplicably both tranquil and intoxicating are revealed, and it's absolutely thrilling. All the regions of our brains that are associated with pleasure must be thrumming.

If I were to represent this cinematically, I would show eight people dancing at a ball in the nineteenth century, when dancers formed two lines facing each other and everyone took turns dancing with everyone else. Except, in my version everyone would also be singing. As each person stepped up to and twirled around another dancer and a new harmony emerged, I'd zoom in on their faces, which would be beaming with unsuppressed joy, as if they were falling in love with every dancer-singer they passed.

"Music has the effect of intensifying or underlining the emotion which a particular event calls forth, by simultaneously co-ordinating the emotions of a group of people," writes Anthony Storr in *Music and the Mind*. Four centuries earlier, a seminarian from the Collegio Germanico wrote almost the exact same thing: "it reduces the natural discord of voices to concord" and "exhibits a certain, more divine harmony." Musically, singing the Agnus Dei is the very embodiment of glory, underlining in the most exquisite way everything the seminarians believed. Therefore, they could sing freely, with sweet longing, reveling in this musical glimpse of what they believed was sure to come.

The composers feel it, too, of course. After writing his *Messiah* in a twenty-four-day whirlwind, Handel said, "I thought I saw all of heaven before me, and the Great God himself." Johannes Brahms described being in a similar thrall. "I felt that I was in tune with the Infinite, and there is no thrill like it." How could it have been any different for Victoria?

"There are eternal truths to be found in this music," writes conductor Jameson Marvin about the works of this period, "truths that when revealed, can provide solace for us, just as this music did for Renaissance citizens hundreds of years ago. I believe that the answer lies in the very elements of the music that engender a transcendent quality for which we yearn—a quality that can provide solace for our souls." According to Marvin those elements are in the mode in which the music was written and in the attention required to master music from this period.

The primary musical modes at the time were Dorian, Phrygian, Lydian, and mixolydian, and each has a particular sound-color. "Dorian sounds serious and has dignity"; Marvin explains, "phrygian sounds sad and mournful; lydian sounds provocative, quasi erotic; by comparison, mixolydian sounds joyful, almost exuberant." The Victoria mass was written in the jubilant mixolydian mode. When I asked John Maclay why he chose this particular mass, he said it was because "it was easy, it was in a bright, joyful key, and it had a lovely eight-voice Agnus Dei that was based on a motet about a vision of Heaven—very angelic in character, and therefore Christmas-y."

However, like Biebl's "Ave Maria," just because a piece is relatively simple, that doesn't mean it's a simple matter to execute it well. Music from this period takes an enormous amount of attention. But the payoff from that kind of collective, close, and sustained attention is immense. Through that sound, Marvin writes, "performers and listeners alike are drawn, in contemplation, to a place of quiet, another world, a place in which energies can be renewed, spirits rejuvenated, souls refreshed."

As I LOOK back and speculate about the feelings of the seminarians, I wonder if Victoria ever tried to see four hundred years into the future. Did it ever cross his mind that the mass originally sung by a choir of twenty Jesuit seminary students would one day be picked up by the likes of me? God knows how many commandments I've broken. Today.

While methods of mass production were still to come, music printing had been around for close to a century in 1576—it's conceivable that Victoria might have pictured copies of his mass lasting long enough to reach a twenty-first-century singer's hands. Still, only a few decades ago, when people tried to imagine the year 2000, they had us flying around in jet packs. Also, considering how devout Victoria was, I don't think he would ever have envisioned a group like ours: over a hundred singers of all faiths and no faiths, the majority of whom were women, many if not most singing his mass just for the sheer joy of it, giving little thought to the music's scared dimension. He would have been like Handel, who when told that his *Messiah* was "a great entertainment," responded, "My lord, I should be sorry if I only entertained them; I wished to make them better."

"Music can affect for good or ill the body as well as the mind," Victoria warned. And, "Nowadays, unfortunately, music does often serve depraved ends." To be honest, sometimes my pleasure *is* a little depraved. Those quiet and careful harmonies separate out and extract a sense of celebration and love in such a focused, distilled form, it can be a heady, sensual experience. It's possible that Victoria would look at our choir and be appalled.

But I don't think so.

Sometimes John e-mails us before a performance; it's like an electronic pep talk. One night his message read, "I don't think you really understand how powerful it is, what you do, what you become, through such intense cooperation toward a common goal. Your energy will blaze brightly for a thousand happy listeners tomorrow, providing a living example of what human beings should aspire to be. . . . A live performance draws listeners and executants alike into an exalted state where, in forgetting our workaday lives, we remember and reconnect with our essential humanity."

In his essay "An Agnostic Response to Christian Art," author Nelson Edmondson (who used Victoria's *Officium Defunctorum* as one of his examples) wrote, "I take satisfaction in belonging to a species of creatures with the ability not only to conceive and perform, but also respond appreciatively to such a work."

If Victoria could somehow witness the effects of his music four centuries later, see the way his mass still excites and unites us, after he recovered from the shock, how could he be anything less than moved that the music from his heart has rung out into the future, where it continues "to reach the ears of the hearers and quietly penetrate their hearts," just as his bishops had commanded all those years ago.

IN THE END, it doesn't take enormous leaps of the imagination to understand in part what the faithful require from music and what is possible. My mother was raised a Catholic. As she lay dying I leaned over her and sang Schubert's version of "Ave Maria." She hadn't been conscious for days and there was little left to do for her but wait. She was in terrible pain at the end, and I'd considered hastening her departure, but no one would tell me the proper dose of morphine and I didn't want to inadvertently cause more suffering. I was relieved to be free from taking that step but still desperate to do something to lessen the seemingly endless and drawn-out torment. Then I remembered how weeks earlier my mother had called me to tell me she'd returned to the church she'd abandoned many years before. She sounded so happy. If taking the church back into her heart was how my mother was going to deal with dying, there was one last thing I could do to help her. I'd already read that music from childhood was the last to go, and Schubert's "Ave Maria" is a sentimental favorite among Catholics. (Bing Crosby sings it in *Going My Way*.) The text comes from a prayer that Catholics say when they are asking Mary to intercede on their behalf. "Ave Maria," it begins, *"gratia plena, Dominus tecum."* "Hail Mary, full of grace, the Lord is with thee." It's what the Angel Gabriel said to Mary and it's meant as words of rejoicing. Gabriel was telling Mary that she was going to give birth to the son of God. But when I sang the words "the Lord is with thee," I was reassuring my mother that she was not alone. I was banking on the ability of the long-familiar melody to get past the morphine and the rapidly disappearing links within her brain to provide some measure of comfort to her still-beating heart—to ease her passing by enhancing her restored beliefs the way only music can.

I would never talk to my mother again. I sang to take her hand one last time. If the music successfully carried those words to a place where she could still hear them, somewhere inside she was saying them along with me. *Holy Mary, Mother of God, pray for us sinners, now and at the hour of our death. Amen.* I don't need to believe a thing about God to understand and feel the hope in those words, those notes. My mother needed to hear them and I needed to believe that she had.

The Last Invocation

Written by Randall Thompson in 1922

Memoranda

Written by Dylan Chan in 2005

**Performed by the Choral Society of Grace Church
in the Spring, 2005**

When I was twenty-four years old I wrote a novel called *God by Twenty-five*. The title came from a joke I'd made. I was managing a telecommunications department, and I'd asked one of the people under me what he wanted to do with his life. He started saying something about becoming a manager, too, and I stopped him. "No, really." I thought he was telling me what he believed I wanted to hear. "What do you want to be by the time you're twenty-five? In your wildest dreams." At the time I thought if you weren't already firmly on the way to making your dreams come true by twenty-five, something was wrong with you. He looked at me funny and insisted that he really wanted to be a manager. I was astounded by his answer. I had dreams of being a rock star, a Nobel Prize–winning author, a movie star, the *New York*

Times star photographer or its star investigative journalist—it was so hard to pick just which kind of star I wanted to be. He must have seen the shock on my face because he immediately asked me, "Why? What do you want to be?" "God," I answered. "I want to be God by twenty-five." I was kidding, of course. I was just trying to suggest that he dream bigger. My joke became the inspiration for the first book I ever wrote, which was not a success. What did I know at twenty-four?

I console myself with the idea that it's natural to be clueless in your twenties, but over the years I've noticed that some of my favorite pieces to sing are frequently from among the composer's earliest works. "Toward the Unknown Region" was one of Ralph Vaughan Williams's first. Tomás Luis de Victoria wrote his *Missa Simile est Regnum Coelorum* when he was twenty-eight. And Randall-freaking-Thompson was only twenty-two when he wrote "The Last Invocation." *And* he finished it in less than a month. It's as though it was already inside him, mature and ready, and it burst from him the minute he picked up a pen.

Perhaps the greatness of "The Last Invocation" is actually due to his extreme youth. The music embodies that first rush of genius, scratched out at a breakneck pace at a time of natural exuberance. Which makes it all the more strange that he chose to write about death. Like Vaughan Williams before him, who also chose to write about death at an early age, Thompson selected his text from Walt Whitman's *Leaves of Grass*.

At the last, tenderly,
From the walls of the powerful, fortress'd house,
From the clasp of the knitted locks—from the keep of the
    well-closed doors,
Let me be wafted.

Let me glide noiselessly forth;
With the key of softness unlock the locks—with a whisper,
Set ope the doors, O soul.

Tenderly! be not impatient!
(Strong is your hold, O mortal flesh,
Strong is your hold, O love).

Thompson dedicated his new composition to his philoso-phy professor George Herbert Palmer, and he presented it to Palmer on his eightieth birthday. I'd love to have seen Palmer's face when he opened up the score to a song about death on the occasion of turning eighty. I can barely read the plea "Let me be wafted" without breaking down. I can't imag-ine how I'd feel at eighty. But obviously Thompson cared for Palmer deeply, and he dedicated the piece to him because he was proud of it. I'm guessing that at twenty-two, Thompson wasn't aware that Palmer might have mixed feelings about the gesture. For the record, Palmer wasn't wafted for another ten years.

Thompson also submitted his new composition to the award committee at Harvard for the annual Boott Prize. The

Boott Prize had been established in 1904 at the behest of composer and Harvard graduate Francis Boott, who left $10,000 to Harvard in order to establish a $100 yearly prize for "the best composition in concerted vocal music." The guidelines for entry aren't very restrictive; the only real requirement is that the winning piece cannot be longer than six minutes in duration. Boott left one piece of advice. "I suggest that the music be neither too ancient nor too modern in style," and if the music was religious he recommended Mozart and Cherubini as models.

"The Last Invocation" didn't win. Even though Thompson had won the Boott Prize three years earlier for a piece nowhere near as evocative or memorable, and the same men were judging in 1922, the committee decided that none of the entries they'd received were worthy of the prize.

Randall Thompson would garner a lot of other recognition that year. He won the John Knowles Paine Traveling Scholarship (awarded for musicology or composition), which he ended up returning in order to accept the Walter Damrosch Fellowship (Frank's brother), which allowed him to study at the American Academy in Rome for the next three years. But it seems that the loss of the Boott stung. George Herbert Palmer contacted one of the committee members, who wrote back that they were all "eagerly even anxiously desirous of giving the prize each year if possible." But each had come to the conclusion that "with all its learning and ardent labor," they couldn't give the prize to "The Last Invocation," adding that each of them "felt strongly that it should be given emphatically honorable mention."

Thompson then wrote to the chairman of the committee, composer Arthur Foote himself. "Recognizing that the composition is not in any sense perfect, it would be a great help to me to know the special defect wh[ich] the committee found, whether vocal, contrapuntal, or artistic. If you would be willing to let me know them do not hesitate to do so in a brief, blunt, way. It will not hurt my feelings—me imperturbe!" ("*Me imperturbe*" is from *Leaves of Grass*.)

"It's not easy to put the finger on the reasons why the prize was not given," Foote responded, "nor have I the right to assume that the others had certain views," but he offered one piece of criticism. "Your counterpoint is free flowing and has gone on since I last saw what you were doing. [Counterpoint refers to the rhythmic and harmonic relationship of the voices to each other.] I think however a dangerous lack results from what appears to be too great concentration on the counterpoint pure and simple and voice parts that are not melodic enough, or interesting by themselves. That is the danger always for us, especially when we get deeply interested in modal counterpoint. The more robust, musical and interesting handling of contrapuntal music [again, he's referring to the relationship between the different melodic lines, which he is saying are not terribly melodic] that one finds in Bach, Verdi, Brahms, Horatio Parker, Mendelssohn, Handel [there's a varied list for you] I think is the prescription."

I was astounded by the "not melodic enough" comment. I'd be less surprised to hear someone suggest that perhaps it's a tad too melodic, veering into the sentimental and indulgent range (although I wouldn't agree). But I'm not a music scholar. I e-mailed Dylan Chan, our former associate conductor and the composer of *Memoranda,* the other piece we sang at the spring concert that year. Dylan was just twenty-seven years old at the time of that concert, and *Memoranda* was his first major piece. What did a fellow young composer (eighty-three years removed) make of Foote's comments?

Foote is "referring to the conflict between the lyricism of an individual vocal line," Dylan e-mailed back, "and counterpoint, which is how those lines interact to generate harmony and musical flow. He apparently felt that in 'The Last Invocation,' Thompson paid too much attention to counterpoint, at the expense of the lyricism and overall musicality of each individual line. As an amateur composer, I can certainly relate. On one hand, there is the temptation to try to make your music too clever, coming up with all sorts of neat contrapuntal techniques, at the expense of what sounds musical (and what is fun and reasonable to sing!); on the other, you can focus too much on melodicism, and have dull counterpoint that does not sustain musical interest.

"For example, have you ever heard Robert Levin's completion of the Mozart *Requiem*?" Mozart died while writing his now famous requiem mass, and the unfinished sections were completed by Franz Xaver Süssmayr, a student of composer

Antonio Salieri's and a friend of Mozart's. If you've heard Mozart's *Requiem,* you've heard the Mozart/Süssmayr version. There is another version, though, and Dylan compared the two. "Levin is the ultimate Mozart scholar, and his completion is the perfect example of meticulous counterpoint that is lacking in lyricism. On the other hand, much of Sussmayr's work is perfectly lyrical (not surprising, because he probably used some of Mozart's original material!), but lacking in contrapuntal complexity." Mozart's contribution, on the other hand, like the Kyrie at the beginning of the *Requiem,* "is perfect in the lyricism of individual lines and in how they weave together to create a coherent, dynamic musical structure."

I asked John what he made of Foote's letter. "Foote betrays his own musical tastes in the composers he cites—all from the Western canon post-Renaissance. I would argue that Foote's list is not so 'varied' as all that, as it basically ignores everything pre-1700, including Randall Thompson's beloved Palestrina. For my own part, I think of 'The Last Invocation' as having a great many beautiful, lyrical lines."

Thompson may not have been as imperturbable as he claimed. After failing to win the Boott Prize, another sixty-one years would pass before "The Last Invocation" was ever performed and it wasn't published until 1989. Perhaps he buried it at the bottom of a drawer. By the time we sang it in 2005, Arthur Foote, who didn't think much of it, is mostly forgotten, and Francis Boott, sadly, is entirely forgotten. Much of

Randall Thompson's music, on the other hand, is performed regularly all over the world.

There is much to love about this one largely neglected piece. In the liner notes for a 1995 recording, Thompson's friend Elliot Forbes, a retired professor of music at Harvard and the former conductor of the Harvard Glee Club and Radcliffe Choral Society, points out two elements of interest about the composition. He mentions the build-up to the climax, when the choir "bursts out with the words, 'Strong is your hold, O mortal flesh!,' sung triple *forte*," and that by the time we sing the last line the dynamics have been reduced to *piano dolce*. "The new feeling of flexibility, of yielding, is there for each listener to interpret on his or her own."

Here is how I interpret it: it is yet another version of "embrace the fall." That line is about dying. Thompson is musically enhancing that line to underscore the idea that we're all going over that cliff, and screaming about it won't get you anywhere. So what is the best way to go? "Let me be wafted." Tenderly. The sopranos repeat the word "tenderly" eight times before singing "At the last, let me be wafted." I sobbed during the climax of the Randall Thompson piece because wafting, like embracing the fall, is bittersweet. There is still a loss that must be transcended.

"The second interest," Forbes continued about "The Last Invocation," "is that it is prophetic in its combination of words and music: an American text is set in the *a cappella* tradition of Renaissance Europe. Thompson's creative journey had started."

His creative journey was also the bulk of our concert that spring. We did three pieces by Thompson and one by Dylan Chan, and all of it was entirely a cappella. When I asked my fellow choristers what they thought of a cappella singing, Christina Davis said, "A cappella is to choral singing as skinny-dipping is to swimming. Vulnerable, exhilarating, and prone to revelations." It feels great, but there are dangers.

"You won't have any instruments to bail you out," John repeatedly warned us. All we had was each other. But that was what would save us, he tried to tell us. "No matter how much you practice," he told us, "no singer in the room can sing choral music on their own. You need each other."

It was to be an exceptionally challenging program. John once said to us before a concert, "Church is about being scared, but an awesome scared. Go out there and terrify people." But on the night of that particular concert we were the ones who were terrified. We also couldn't wait.

Dylan Chan, on the other hand, was scared on a whole other level. We were about to premiere his most ambitious composition and we'd had only seven rehearsals, most of which were focused on the Randall Thompson pieces. To make matters worse, Dylan's music was not only different from what we normally sang, it felt different every time we rehearsed it. "For other pieces that I had conducted for the Choral Society," Dylan told me, "I had a very good sense of what I thought things should sound like, and what they would sound like, from recordings or prior performances. But for *Memoranda,* I had none of that." Internally, he knew the music well, but hearing it out loud, "There were sounds and feeling in it that were totally unexpected, parts that didn't sound anything like what I had planned."

The biggest problem was the tempo. Influenced by both hip-hop and Renaissance polyphony, Dylan wanted to rely on rhythm, rather than harmony or melody, to establish the emotional center of the piece. It was very forward-thinking of him considering all the recent research suggesting that rhythm is a critical component of emotional expression in music. But Dylan hadn't settled on exactly what tempo to take, and in rehearsal we felt unstable and unsure. In a piece where rhythm was going to be used to express the beating heart of the composition, we were hearts in distress.

Memoranda consists of three movements, all of which contain the words dead or death. But like most songs about death, each is really about resurrection in one form or another. Dylan hoped to get around death by showing us that music would never die. The text of the first movement comes from a poem by Emily Dickinson.

A word is dead
When it is said,
Some say.

I say it just
Begins to live
That day.

As with all the poems he chose for his piece, Dylan had first read "A Word Is Dead" in high school. At the time, he thought learning it was mostly a dry, academic exercise. "That's what most people probably think of a lot of classical music, too," he said. It wasn't that he didn't think the poems were great; he did. It's why he came back to them years later. "But what I love about art," he went on, "is that the artist who created the work of art is only half of the story. By setting these poems to music, and then performing them together, they live on. They remain alive. We are the ones who make art live on—we, by performing it, give it new life."

The next movement of his piece comes from the poet-of-choice among composers, Walt Whitman. It's the death carol from his elegy for Abraham Lincoln, "When lilacs last in the dooryard bloom'd."

> Come, lovely and soothing death,
> Undulate round the world serenely arriving, arriving.
> In the day, in the night, to all, to each,
> Sooner or later, delicate Death.

Once again we come to a battle you can't win—we're all going to die—so how does one embrace this final fall? "Whitman's poetry in general is the greatest embodiment of words giving forth life," Dylan said, cheating death "through the energy and vitality of the words." This particular piece is also "a wonderfully musical poem, with a rhythm vitality so characteristic of Whitman's best work. I attempted to preserve as

much of the inherent poetic meter as possible, leading to a
highly irregular but clear and propulsive rhythm, resulting
in a dance macabre that mirrors the sentiment of the text."
In other words, when you come to this final battle, instead of
fighting, lay down your weapons and sway right into the arms
of the enemy.

The text for the last movement is from another Emily
Dickinson poem.

> Because I could not stop for Death,
> He kindly stopped for me;
> The carriage held but just ourselves
> And Immortality.
>
> . . . .
>
> We paused before a house that seemed
> A swelling of the ground;
> The roof was scarcely visible,
> The cornice but a mound.
>
> Since then 'tis centuries, and yet each
> Feels shorter than the day
> I first surmised the horses' heads
> Were toward eternity.

In order to give life to death in this movement, Dylan borrowed a trick from Mozart. Dylan had decided that the final
chord on the last word of the piece—*eternity*—needed to
"convey openness; you don't know whether it is supposed to

be a major chord or minor chord; you expect it to go on, to live on." He'd been listening to Mozart's *Requiem* at the time, and he saw that "the Kyrie ends with a big open fifth (D-A), then goes straight on to the Dies irae movement. It's one of the most dramatic moments in all of music. You just had this super-intense buildup through the Requiem and Kyrie, which ends on this massive cadence leading to the open fifth, which you expect to be a final chord, but instead it keeps on going, spilling into the even more intense Dies irae movement which follows. Traditionally, cadences like that end with a major chord, which gives much more of a sense of finality and resolution. The fact that it was an open fifth, and not a completed major or minor chord, is significant. Your mind is thinking, 'is it going to keep on going? where is this going to go?' It feels like it could keep on going in a loop for all of eternity. That was what I was thinking for the end of *Memoranda*. I wanted it to feel settled and unsettled at the same time. I wanted people to think about what would come next, to feel like it wasn't over."

That is quite a transcendent feat, and it wasn't at all clear that either the music or our voices were up to it. Dylan's piece was tricky, and so we practiced with the piano and not a cappella. "As late as two weeks before the concert," John told me, "Dylan and I both had our doubts about whether we would be able to wean you all off the piano for his pieces." While they hoped we'd rise to the occasion, it was getting down to the wire. Dylan was also having qualms about his ability to conduct his own work. In the very last few days leading up to the concert, he continued to have misgivings, and he and John agreed that if needed, John would step in and conduct, even on the spot.

At the dress rehearsal the night before the concert we had a such a shaky run-through under Dylan's direction that John had no choice but to take the baton and "rather forcefully beat it into the group."

On the night of the concert, Dylan was still undecided. He wasn't confident that even if he summoned the courage to take the baton, he'd be able to control us. He was still working out just what he wanted the piece to sound like, and without that settled, he'd never be able to lead. You can't communicate with any kind of clarity or strength something that is not in your own head. Right up until the moment when he made up his mind and stepped up to the podium, it was all just one big question mark.

I imagine it like that movie cliché, when all the words that most terrify the protagonist keep repeating in a voice-over. There are two Randall Thompson quotes that could easily have been echoing in Dylan's ears. "In order to succeed, a choral composer has to make his emotional intent crystal clear." "If a piece is too difficult for amateurs to sing, the chances are that it is not good enough." When Dylan turned to face us on the night of the concert, he was plainly scared. But he'd embraced the fall. He voluntarily walked up to the edge of that cliff and he was going over. He no longer had any choice about that.

I can still see his face when he raised his baton. Excitement and fear all at once. I did the only thing I could for him in that moment, I smiled at him. I'm pretty sure almost everyone in the choir did the same. He wasn't just a composer, he was *our* composer and we were all going over that cliff together. "That's the great thing about choral conducting," he e-mailed me later, "you get to see everyone's eyes, and faces, and smiles." Dylan shut out the nine hundred people behind him and opened his eyes and his heart to the people in front of him. "I knew that everyone was on my side, that we would all work together to make this piece work. Seeing everyone's face before, during, and after the performance was one of the most heartwarming, inspiring, and exhilarating experiences of my musical career." It must be something every conductor realizes at some point. We want you to do well. We're here for you.

"I stood in the second row of the choir," John later told me, "hiding behind the organ, singing (sometimes other parts' entrances) but ready to spring to the podium if necessary." In the end it wasn't. "It was as good as anything else on the program," said bass Tim Bohn. "It must be the way Mozart or Haydn or Vaughan Williams felt the first time a composition they had written was brought to life by a chorus," Peter Julian added. "Seeing the look on Dylan's face as he conducted us moved me nearly to tears."

For some, it was more than nearly. "When he conducted," Wendy Hayden recalled, "it was as if he massaged each note into your heart. Everyone around me had tears in their eyes after singing this piece." But Wendy's tears fell because that night when she looked out into the audience while singing Dylan's piece, she felt as though she saw her friend Jim, who had died more than ten years before. They'd met in college and were very much in love, but he wanted to stay in St. Louis and she wanted to move to New York. They parted. Years later, when she found out he'd divorced, they got together for a reunion in Chicago, "our favorite place," Wendy told me. "I felt like I was in a movie; he gave me a box of letters that I had written and together we reread every word." They met whenever they could after that. "Finally he came to New York for my very first concert at Grace Church, in 1994. We had a fabulous weekend, he left on Sunday, and I got a call on Tuesday telling me he crashed into a tree and died on Monday night."

"I thought I would never sing again," Wendy said. "As a society, we don't really talk about death or confront it in a constructive way." But the choir helped her heal.

And now something about the character of Dylan's composition brought Jim back after all those years. It made her finally become fully aware of something she hadn't completely understood at the time of his death. "Jim had already stepped back from life and was not fully engaged in activity. He was looking at art and architecture in the city as if he wouldn't see it again. He made several remarks about all he wanted was this very moment." When Wendy sang *Memoranda,* "I was able to put myself in his shoes and think: I do understand how you were feeling. The journey to New York City was to say good-bye. 'Come lovely and soothing death' was in your eyes." Wendy knew Jim would have wanted her to continue and to be happy, and "so I sang to him and for him" and cried.

THAT SUMMER HURRICANE Katrina almost decimated New Orleans. I stopped watching the coverage when they interviewed a guy who had killed his dog rather than leave it on the roof to die slowly and alone when the helicopter pilot refused to let him take the dog onto the helicopter. That same summer I made the mistake of listening to the 9/11 tape of Melissa Doi pleading with the 911 operator to send help faster. "There's no one here yet and the floor is completely engulfed. We're on the floor and we can't breathe. And it's very, very, very hot." I don't know why I listened to it. "I'm going to die. I know I am," she said to the operator. She did. I also made the mistake of reading about Eliza Jumel, a nineteenth-century New York semisocialite who lived a sad, Miss Havisham–like existence in Washington Heights before dying alone. *That's going to be me.* At the end of the year I went to West Virginia to research and write a story about a family who lost five of their children in a fire on Christmas day in 1945.

Death is everywhere and inescapable. Society may not talk about it, but composers do. The music we sing every year comes right out and says it: either the end is coming or it's right here. "We do not doubt," a 1977 Grace Church newsletter read, "that there are needs which run deeper than words, deeper even than thought, and that some of them may be reached by the power of music." Music steeped in sorrow can sometimes be the very thing to help us get past seemingly unbearable grief. "It feels as if I am tapping into an untouched emotional territory of loss," Wendy said about singing, "then feelings of contentment come shining through."

"You're never more alive than when you're singing about death," Barbara remembers about that night. "I appreciated Dylan's pieces because the poems were worthy. You felt like you were singing about something important because the words were important. Singing the poems was another way of getting the point across."

Music critic Henry Krehbiel wrote, "To sing in a choir is the quickest, surest, and best way to become intimate with music, to get close to the seat of its emotional life, where its heart-throbs can be felt and heard . . . to hold communion with its gentle saints and glorious heroes." Composers have been and always will be my glorious heroes. If the piece is right they can provide hope, solace, and sometimes they can even resurrect the dead. On any given concert night, just as Wendy saw Jim, people from the choir are looking out into the audience of Grace Church and seeing faces of those who are no longer with us. "One of my oldest friends came to hear us sing the Mozart *Requiem*," Barbara told me. Then the woman died. "The next time we sang it she wasn't there. But I could still see her sitting out there."

I'm sure no one has ever said "dream bigger" to Dylan Chan, as I did to that young man all those years ago. When Dylan wrote *Memoranda,* he wanted nothing less than to be able to cheat death, and on that night, like many composers before him, he did.

And music about the end, death, even if it's all just a beautiful trick, doesn't have to be so sad. It is, after all, a celebration of what we deeply cherish. Despite all the disappointments I've had, I still want to live forever and I do everything I can to remain healthy. Singing is one of those things. I also eat well and exercise every day. A few years after this concert I joined a city gym near me because it has a pool. I hadn't been swimming for decades, but when I was growing up, during the summer I was in either a pool or the Long Island Sound every day.

A few weeks after I'd started swimming again, when it no longer killed me to swim laps, I slid down underneath the water, braced my feet against the side of the pool, then pushed as hard as I could and took off for my next lap. It's my favorite part. For those first few feet as you surge forward underwater, before you break the surface again, you feel like a rocket taking off into another world, but in slow motion, as the water gently softens what would otherwise have been an explosive burst. In that brief pocket of stretched-out time, as I soared, *adagietto,* through the bright blue, enveloping water,

I immediately remembered the line "Let me be wafted." If such a departure from life is possible, I thought, this is what it would be like. Please let it be like this. Embracing that final fall won't be nearly so terrifying if it's anything like this. And then I dove over and over into the sparkling blue universe, gliding back and forth, and back and forth, each time staying underneath the water as long as I could, with Thompson's luminous and radiant music sounding in my head, until, as always, I eventually ran out of breath.

Recitative
Francis Boott and R. Nathaniel Dett

I went up to Harvard to learn more about Francis Boott, the composer who established the award that Randall Thompson didn't win for *The Last Invocation*. I was touched by the almost complete absence of information out there about Boott's life, and I felt an overwhelming need to recover him. The folder I found containing his papers, though, was sadly slim and almost everything inside was as dispiriting as the meagerness of the file. There were a lot of newspaper clippings about his death in 1904, and a reprint of the memorial address given by his friend the famed psychologist William James, who said of Boott, "shy and sensitive, craving praise as every normal human being craves it, yet getting little, he had, I think, a certain consciousness of living in the shadow." The fact that one of Boott's final gestures was to see to it that the young composers who came after him were not similarly consigned to the shadows made me want to retrieve him even more.

But soon after Boott died, what little trace of him remained began to disappear. The Boott family mansion where he'd grown up on Cambridge Street was torn down and replaced by the Ambassador Hotel. His more popular songs quickly fell out of style, and while the Harvard Glee Club continued to sing his rousing "Here's a Health to King Charles" for many years, no one could recall who had written it. There was a time when Boott was a familiar figure in Harvard Square, setting out from the family mansion twice daily in his long, stylish cape. But by 1949, except for a few aging neighbors, no one knew that someone's home had once stood in the spot the hotel now occupied, or remembered the family who had lived within. In that relatively brief stretch of time, Boott had become less than a ghost.

He'd fought hard against disappearing, regularly transcending sad events that might have flattened others. First, a stepfather who had banished him from love and music to a school so grim it could have been the model for the Lowood school in *Jane Eyre*. Later, a beloved wife who died after only a few years of marriage, leaving him with an eighteen-month-old daughter, Lizzie. Boott had originally planned to leave the child with his sister, but luckily his plan didn't work out. After sailing with Lizzie and her wet nurse to Italy, where his family was then living, "we three again resumed our wanderings," and his daughter became his whole life. When he died someone wrote, "Old dwellers in Florence grew familiar with the sight of the handsome American carrying his daughter on his arm while she was still an infant, and afterward with her always at his side." Boott immersed himself in Lizzie's education, introducing her to music, art, and languages. They must have made an elegant picture when he read to her from a fourth-century Latin translation of the Bible while she drew or painted.

Boott was known to all the siblings in William James's family, and each had an opinion about how he was raising Lizzie. Alice James, for instance, did not approve. All this education was largely a waste of time, she thought. He should be getting her ready for matrimony. Exasperated in general by his impractical approach to life, she later wrote, "He is more of a child than most infants of six. . . ." But apparently he was a child she couldn't quite resist, because she also added, "He is so handsome & frank & honest, that one can't but forgive him all his absurdities till the next time he provokes you. . . ." Novelist Henry James, on the other hand, appreciated the woman that Lizzie had become, describing her as "the infinitely civilized and sympathetic, the markedly produced Lizzie." The relationship between father and daughter inspired the characters Gilbert and Pansy Osmand in James's novel *Portrait of a Lady* and later, Adam and Maggie in *The Golden Bowl.*

Despite Alice's worries, Lizzie grew up to become an accomplished artist and caught the eye of painter Frank Duveneck. After an engagement that lasted years, they married. But in a horrible repetition of what happened to her mother, two years later she was dead, leaving her husband with a toddler, in this case a son named Frank. A devastated Francis Boott left Florence, the city where he had been so happy, and returned to Cambridge. He'd somehow convinced his son-in-law to send his grandson to be raised by relatives in Boston, but Boott and Frank were never close.

Boott lived on sixteen more years, and while he continued to make friends and write music, including a song for Lizzie, which while not sad—"Joy of the morning, Darling of morning, Blithe little, lithe little daughter of mine"—it nonetheless made clear that life for Boott was not quite as felicitous as it had once been. Still, he didn't harbor any bitterness or regret. He embraced the fall. Before he died in 1904, he made arrangements for the Boott Prize, a generous final gesture from an already fading composer. He also made a list of songs for a fourth and last album to be published. The words of one (text by Dr. Silas Weir Mitchell) embody a serene acceptance, and a hope similar to Whitman's "Let me be wafted."

I know the night is near at hand,
The mists lie low on hill and bay,
The autumn sheaves are dew-less dry,
But I have had, have had the day.
Yes, I have had, dear Lord, the day;
When at Thy call I have the night,
Brief be the twilight as I pass
From light to dark, from dark to light.

At the end of Boott's memorial service, William James concluded his address with: "Good-by, then, old friend. . . . in that wider world of being of which this little Cambridge world of ours forms so infinitesimal a part, we may be sure that all our spirits and their missions here will continue in some way to be represented, and that ancient human loves will never lose their own."

"Here's a Health to King Charles" was cut from the Harvard song book in the mid-1960s. When I contacted the only surviving child of Boott's grandson Frank, a daughter named Hope, she told me that she'd never heard of the Boott Prize. And while Boott wished for Frank to continue in the study of music that he'd begun, Frank went into engineering. Today no one in the family seems to know, or has ever sung, any of Boott's songs.

The long list of Boott Prize winners, however, continues to grow, and there are at least a few familiar names in addition to Randall Thompson, including one particularly interesting winner, Robert Nathaniel Dett, who won in 1920 for his setting of the spiritual "Don't Be Weary Traveler." Dett was African American, and he won at a time when most of America was segregated and black music had long been belittled in minstrel shows. Between 1919, when Dett had started writing "Don't Be Weary Traveler," and 1922, 239 blacks were lynched in America.

Dett was also a summer school student, thirty-seven years old, and actually pretty far along in his career as a composer and an academic when Harvard awarded him the Boott Prize.

He'd been named the director of music at the Hampton Institute, in Virginia, in 1913. Summers for Dett were not for
relaxing, it seems, but for absorbing more music and education, and after grabbing the prize he was back at the Institute,
where by the time he left in 1932 he'd founded the School of
Music, the Hampton Choral Union, the Musical Arts Society,
and the Hampton Institute Choir.

The "weary traveler" in Dett's winning motet is a refer-
ence to the slaves on their journey to freedom along Harriet
Tubman's Underground Railroad. Dett had grown up immersed in Underground Railroad history. He was born in
1882 in Drummondsville, Ontario, which had a large population of blacks descended from escaped slaves, and eleven years
later his family moved to the last stop on the Underground
Railroad—Niagara Falls. Dett must have been raised on har-
rowing tales of slaves running for their lives and on the music
that evolved to comfort them and give them strength. For his
entire life Dett was committed to elevating the cultural heri-
tage of black music. Before leaving Harvard he was awarded
one other prize, the Bowdoin, for an essay titled "The Emancipation of Negro Music."

Dett was expanding on a theme he'd written about two
years earlier. "We have this wonderful store of folk music—the
melodies of an enslaved people, who poured out their longing,
their griefs, and their aspirations in the one great universal
language. But this store will be of no value unless we utilize
it, unless we treat it in such manner that it can be presented

in choral form, in lyric and operatic works, in concertos and suites and salon music—unless our musical architects take the rough timber of Negro themes and fashion from it music which will prove that we, too, have national feelings and characteristics. . . ."

Six years after winning the Boott Prize, Dett wrote another motet inspired by the weary traveler, this time using the words of a spiritual titled "Let Us Cheer the Weary Traveler." According to Dett biographer Anne Key Simpson, this spiritual was "widely used by the slaves as a signal that one of their number was being helped to escape to freedom. . . ." Although Dett lived at a time of lynchings, when people snapped pictures of them for postcards, he remained positive throughout his life. In 1940 he addressed a group of black students at Bennett College in North Carolina, where segregation was still legal. "If you, from your experiences which have been much richer than mine, will contribute literature characterized by the spirit of hope found in the spiritual, you will be an inspiration to the composers of our group and a new day for the Negro will dawn." Three years later, after a long and productive career, Dett died of a heart attack while traveling with the USO women's chorus, which he had helped train.

BOOTT, WHO'D LIVED through the Civil War, once wrote, "Some one has said that slavery has been an incalculable benefit to the black race, but, if so, what must the disease have been for which such treatment is a remedy?" When Dett was just starting out in life, and beginning his first year of music study at the Oberlin Conservatory, and Boott was at the end of his, preparing his legacy, the civil rights activist W. E. B. Du Bois published his book of essays *The Souls of Black Folk*. At the end of the chapter titled "Of the Sorrow Songs," he wrote:

> If somewhere in this whirl and chaos of things there dwells Eternal Good, pitiful yet masterful, then anon in His good time America shall rend the Veil and the prisoned shall be free. Free, free as the sunshine trickling down the morning into these high windows of mine, free as yonder fresh young voices welling up to me from the caverns of brick and mortar below—welling with song, instinct with life, tremulous treble and darkening bass. My children, my little children, are singing to the sunshine, and thus they sing:
>
> Let us cheer the weary traveller,
> Cheer the weary traveller,
> Let us cheer the weary traveller
> Along the heavenly way.
>
> And the traveller girds himself, and sets his face toward the Morning, and goes his way.

In 1998 the Nathaniel Dett Chorale was founded in Canada to feature Afrocentric choral music. When Barack Obama was elected the forty-fourth president of the United States, The Smithsonian hosted a three-day festival to celebrate his inauguration. The Chorale was invited to participate. On the last day of the festival, as Obama paraded by, the group stood on the steps of the Canadian Embassy and serenaded him with Dett's motet, "Let Us Cheer the Weary Traveler."

As Obama made his way to the steps of the Capitol to be sworn in as America's first black president, he moved forward into a place in history with Dett's music of encouragement ringing in the air, proving, as William James had said at Boott's memorial all those years ago, "that all our spirits and their missions here will continue in some way to be represented, and that ancient human loves will never lose their own."

O Magnum Mysterium

Written by Morten Lauridsen in 1994

**Performed by the Choral Society of Grace Church
most recently in the Winter, 2008**

It happened in an old church in Limberg, Germany. After the choir sang "O Magnum Mysterium," an elderly gentlemen walked up to the composer, Morten Lauridsen, and said, "They will be singing that piece for thousands of years." It was the best thing he could have said. For centuries, great composers such as Giovanni Pierluigi da Palestrina, Tomás Luis de Victoria, and William Byrd have been setting this particular chant to music, and their versions are so stirring and transcendent that people continue to sing them today. When Lauridsen's interpretation premiered in 1994, Paul Salamunovich of the Los Angeles Master Chorale turned around and, for the first time in his choral conducting career, spoke directly to the audience. If anyone had asked him who his favorite composer was, he told them, he would have said Tomás Luis de Victoria. Victoria's "O Magnum Mysterium" remains as fresh as the day it was written. "Tonight, you're about to hear the world premiere of the twentieth-century counterpart," he told the audience. "A piece so beautiful," he said, it would go on to outperform every American choral piece ever written. With those words he turned around, raised his baton, and roughly six minutes later, at fifty-one years old, Morten Lauridsen had his first genuine blockbuster. He'd written pieces that moved people before, but "O Magnum Mysterium" was a shot of adrenaline straight to the heart. In three short years, the music would become the Theodore Presser Company's highest-selling choral piece since its founding in 1783. As it raced around the world, each concert generating still more concerts, people were singing Lauridsen's chorus more than any other piece by an American choral composer, just as Paul Salamunovich had predicted.

Lauridsen would later admit it was the most difficult piece he'd ever written. Commissioned by Los Angeles Master Chorale board member Marshall Rutter in honor of his wife, Terry Knowles, the text comes from the matins (prayers) of Christmas. The entire chant consists of just two lines, with one word, *alleluia,* at the end.

O magnum mysterium, et admirabile sacramentum, ut
    animalia viderent Dominum natum, jacentem in praesepio!
Beata Virgo, cujus viscera meruerunt portare Dominum
    Christum. Alleluia.

That translates to:

O great mystery, and wonderful sacrament, that animals
    should see the newborn Lord, lying in a manger!
Blessed is the Virgin whose womb was worthy to bear Christ
    the Lord. Alleluia!

The meaning couldn't be simpler or more direct. But it's one thing to communicate a range and depth of emotion when you have an entire symphony or oratorio to pull it off; it's quite another when you have only a few minutes and two lines of text. As if this weren't daunting enough, Lauridsen decided to add one more objective: the second line of his piece would embody the entirety of Mary's experience, from the birth of Christ to his appalling death on the cross. He would represent Mary's "significance and suffering" in the breadth of one single line.

To accomplish this, Lauridsen went back to a remote island where he'd been spending his summers since he was a boy, and a cabin without electricity or running water that he'd bought in the early 1970s. Originally part of a general store, the cabin was built in the early 1900s and had already been abandoned for twenty-five years when Lauridsen purchased it. In the winter the place looks like it might collapse under the weight of the snow. But what might seem to some like a spartan setting was magical to Lauridsen, perhaps evoking the sense of sanctuary that arises from this piece. He sat down in front of a modest fifty-dollar spinet piano and got to work.

Lauridsen wanted the music to be as straightforward and uncomplicated as the text. "I started with a mountainful of notes," he told me in a telephone interview, "and ended with something you could fit in your hand." To distill the piece to its emotional essence, Lauridsen drew inspiration from a painting, *Still Life with Lemons, Oranges and a Rose,* Francisco de Zurbarán's homage to the Virgin Mary. In a 2009 *Wall Street Journal* article, Lauridsen wrote how with only a few objects, "The painting projects an aura of mystery, powerful in its unadorned simplicity, its mystical quality creating an atmosphere of deep contemplation." Lauridsen wanted to match de Zurbarán brush stroke for note, to have the most profound effect with the simplest possible setting, and to "create, as Zurbarán had in paint, a deeply-felt religious statement, at once uncomplicated and unadorned yet powerful and transformative in its effect upon the listener." Six months later Paul Salamunovich was holding the new composition in his hands. Lauridsen had been so successful and so clear in his directions, Salamunovich said, "I could feel what he wanted from it," after only one reading.

"There'd been a lot of buzz about the piece from the singers," Lauridsen said. One night he drove over to the rehearsal to hear how it was coming along. After listening to them sing, he stumbled out to the parking lot and just sat there in his car. He'd long ago chosen to compose for the voice precisely because it was "the most personal instrument." Now those voices had, with his own music, taken hold of his very soul. "You see, we can envision what the piece will sound like, and I know to some degree what it will sound like, but to hear all the different voice colors, done by this world-class ensemble . . ." and here Lauridsen stopped for a moment, struggling to find the right words. "It had a deep effect on me. It did exactly what I had aimed for in all those countless hours of trying to flesh out this piece and to deal with these words." He'd wanted his piece to have a transformative effect on the listener, and it did. That night the listener was the composer himself. At the premiere the audience went crazy.

"I HAD A bass next to me the second time we sang it," Choral Society alto Mary Horenkamp told me, "and he was new or in his second year with us. He turned to me afterwards and said, 'That was amazing!' We both admitted to getting choked up while singing it." When tenor Milton Justice sang it for the first time, he looked down at the music in his hands and said to those around him, "I want this sung at my funeral." A morbid reaction perhaps, but Milton had immediately recognized it as music to accompany one into eternity. Everyone knew what he meant and what he was feeling. A number of people in the choir have let me know that Lauridsen's "O Magnum Mysterium" is one of their favorite pieces to sing. Part of the reason for that, Lauridsen—a former singer himself—believes, is that he made sure every voice part got something great to do. "I want to make this music gracious for the singer, I want people to say I can't wait to do this Lauridsen piece because the guy writes elegant lines for me." In many choral pieces, sopranos get the melody, and sometimes the other voices are little more than back-up. I remember one singer complaining about a piece we sang at Christmas: "Try being an alto in that one. So freaking boring. You park on one note and then just stay there."

But Lauridsen has great affection for all the voice parts, and altos in particular, it appears. "Altos! The great overlooked voice. Not in my music!" he happily proclaimed over the phone. Then he proudly told me that there's a group of altos in Ames, Iowa, who celebrate his birthday every year. That has to be at least in part because he gave the most important moment in his most famous and successful piece to them.

It comes at the climax, on the word *virgo* (virgin). "I wanted to portray somehow what Mary had gone through," seeing her son on the cross, to shine a "sonic flashlight" on that moment and in that moment "communicate harmonically all her pain and suffering." Lauridsen spent untold hours stripping away what he had written until he found the purist expression of that sorrow. In the end it came on a single note, a G-sharp, which he gave to the altos. "It's the only note in the entire piece that's out of key, creating a certain kind of dissonance," and "That sadness, on the word *virgo*, indicates to me the poignancy and sadness that Mary must have felt about bearing the . . . loss of her son."

In interviews, Lauridsen frequently recalls how his love of music began with the sound of his mother's singing. I tried to find out if that first voice, sadly silenced in 1997, was an alto, but he wouldn't answer. Perhaps that's because if the voice is the most personal instrument, a mother's voice is the most personal of all. I asked because a sense of sadness runs all through "O Magnum Mysterium." It's a strangely beautiful and affecting sadness, and it's there from beginning to end, even when we're singing alleluia. For me, the music is saying that no matter what there is to celebrate, there's always this tragedy, this suffering underneath. Or, equally true, no matter what tragedy occurs, there is always reason for joy. In the end, Lauridsen didn't manage to convey the breadth of Mary's significance and suffering in one line, or even one note. It's in every note. And altos aren't the only ones who love it. My soprano friend Barbara told me that the Victoria setting of the "O Magnum Mysterium" was the first choral piece she'd ever learned and that she loved it dearly. "I was prepared to not like the Lauridsen and of course ended up loving it and thinking that the *beata virgo* part was about the most beautiful music I'd ever sung in my life!"

When asked point blank in a radio interview about what is it about his music that goes so deep inside us, Lauridsen admitted, "I don't know. We strive to go to those places, whether you're a composer, sculptor, or a dancer. We try to go to those places that are beyond words, that cannot be explained. For me these are very sacred places, when you experience something that is so profound that there is no way you can begin to express it through words, or really by any other means. Occasionally, as artists, we reach that spot."

In his *Wall Street Journal* piece, Lauridsen wrote about the devices he uses to take us there. "The piece seems to float, to hover in the air, due to a predominant use of inverted chords. . . ." I ran back to John for an explanation. Inverted chords, he explained, "refers to the inversion of a triad." A simple C major chord—C, E, G—becomes E-G-C, then G-C-E, which "creates a sort of rootlessness as you never have the root of the chord on the bottom." Until you get back to the original C major chord, you have that sense of floating. John believes Lauridsen is evoking the mysteriousness of the event, and he is almost certainly correct. For me, though, this is also the only reasonable position to take in a world of sorrow: you do your best to float above it, in serene contemplation if possible. It is yet another version of embracing the fall. When faced with something you can't change, change your response to it. Perhaps I was seeing this outlook everywhere because of my own need, but the year before, in my ongoing quest for embrace-the-fall skills, I learned to do something called mindfulness meditation. Every note of Lauridsen's piece, coupled with the text, seemed to evoke this particular form of focus that I'd learned.

The point of this style of meditation is not to try to change your life or yourself, but instead be more aware of everything going on in that moment; what you're thinking; what you're feeling physically and emotionally. My thoughts frequently run along the lines of, "God, I am such a jerk, why am I always a jerk," but when I'm meditating, instead of trying to stop these thoughts, the fact that I'm judging myself in this way is simply added to the list of things I'm observing. Once you have a handle on what is going on with yourself, you're supposed to open up to what is going on around you, to sights, sounds, and scents.

If I'm lucky, in addition to those "I'm a jerk" voices, I'll slowly start to hear the chorus of the city: birds, metallic clanking, airplanes, helicopters, the sounds of cars in the distance which then come closer, closer, then a whoosh as each car recedes. It is quite a cacophony, but it's surprisingly soothing and also remarkably well orchestrated. Somehow the cooing of pigeons comes through even when it's surrounded by the din of concrete-pulverizing jackhammers. My self-loathing is also still there, but it's in the background now, the clamor of my emotions orchestrated as expertly as the sounds of the city.

The only other time I'm present in this way is when I'm singing, and I become superconscious of the voices surrounding me. In those moments I have that same high-definition appreciation of everything that's going on. One second I'm in a room with 152 separate individuals, and the next, everyone's heart is beating as one, and I can also hear every voice, every sound, from someone's foot scraping the floor to the rustling of programs. Lauridsen's simple and meditative two-line piece induces this same mindful, transcendent state; it's music that does not seek to change. The Virgin Mary couldn't save her son from the cross. But Lauridsen's all-encompassing composition tenderly weaves together both her suffering and her bliss into exactly what Lauridsen aimed for when he wrote it: "a quiet song of profound inner joy." When we sing it, it's like a guided group meditation.

On NPR recently, a Benedictine monk described chanting with his fellow monks and learning to live as a community in the singing. "When I'm really giving my best self to the chanting in the church, my whole body relaxes, my voice takes on a different resonance, but more importantly within the mind there's a peacefulness that can come there and allows me simply to center myself within the divine; and that's a physical effect, that if I pay attention to it I can feel it happening in my body."

When I asked our current associate conductor, Tony Bellomy, to name his favorite piece to lead (associate conductors sometimes take the baton), he immediately answered, "It would have to be the Lauridsen 'O Magnum Mysterium.'" Elizabeth Abrams remembers the night Tony conducted it. "At the end—the silence—it was longer than usual, as if none of us or Tony or the audience wanted it to end." I remember the silence. I was holding my breath. There are always a few moments of stillness before applause begins, but this was different, more reverent, and I remember it going on for an unusually long time, as well. "Tony closed his eyes," Elizabeth continued, "brought his hands down, and still, there was that beat of silence. I felt all of us in the church were connected for a moment in a very profound way. Then, Tony opened his eyes and mouthed, 'thank you.' The audience burst into applause. "It was one of those extraordinary few seconds that I'll remember forever."

Mary Horenkamp agreed. "Watching Tony is so spiritual. He always seems to be conducting from another realm, and his gentle hand movements gather us together and cradle us into that realm. I love Tony on that plane of existence." Tony's hand movements are so hypnotic even a cellist in the orchestra had become mesmerized by them. He went up to Tony afterward to tell him that it was amazing to watch his hands, "there was so much music in them."

I'll never forget that or Tony's conducting. Soprano Nancy Tepper, who has sung with many other musical groups over the years, said, "Trust me when I say we are blessed to have Tony. He is so much more than the normal accompanist that most groups have." I recently learned that Tony has degrees in piano performance and vocal accompanying and since 2009 has been conducting for the New York Lyric Opera Theatre. "Because of him," Nancy concluded, "we sing better as a group." Which makes it all the more strange to admit that prior to that concert, during rehearsals, when Tony is working as our accompanist, I barely gave him a thought. What is there to think about? Accompanists play the piano during rehearsals, they're very good, and the better they are, the more invisible they are. They are the unsung heros of the choral world.

TONY CAME TO the choir as a singer in 2005, after moving to New York four months earlier. He joined for the same reasons a lot of people join: "I wanted friends!" It seems like an excellent motive now, but when I joined the Choral Society I was trying to stave off depression brought on by a string of romantic disappointments. After quickly determining that the choir didn't offer a lot of dating options for me, I stopped giving the social side of the choir much thought.

"I used to joke with John that he needed to get more straight guys in the choir," Lucia Rivieccio admitted to me, "and he would insist that the majority of men *were* straight. Then it became, Okay, straight, but not married. One year, after debating this one night, I got an e-mail from him at 2 a.m., where he had worked it all out statistically, in his John way, to prove to me that there were more straight men than I thought in the choir. I still tease him about that."

Whatever their orientation, I began to look forward to seeing the same faces week after week. When people left the choir I was sad. Not long ago Daniel Alling, a bass, stood up at the end of rehearsal to say good-bye. He was moving back to Sweden and before he left there was something he wanted to say. "If you ever move to another country," he told us, "join a choir. Choir people are the nicest people in the world and you people show that." Tony echoed those words.

"What better place to find friends than in doing something I love so much." It has taken me a while, but what I considered a fringe benefit—friends—has become one of the most important things about choral singing and it is inseparable from the music.

Which makes what happened to Tony next all the more poignant. A year after he'd joined, John asked Tony to become our accompanist, replacing Dylan Chan, who was leaving for his residency in California. Tony, who had years of experience rehearsing, conducting, and playing with choral groups, said yes. But agreeing meant sacrificing so soon something he had come to treasure. He'd have to leave the ranks and new friends he'd only just made, to sit at the piano in the center of the room. Alone. "I absolutely love the work I do with the choir now," Tony told me, "and wouldn't trade it for anything. But when I think about my first year in choir, I miss the camaraderie felt when sitting in the middle of the group, experiencing the same perspective as everyone else and getting to know the people around me in my quartet."

As Tony sits there, alone, he must not only become hyperaware of all the people not thinking about him, he has to maintain an almost constant, near-telepathic connection with John. John has been busy getting into the head of the composer and working out how to communicate that to us. Tony has to get into the composer's head, the choir's, *and* John's. He not only has to interpret what he's seeing from John and "translate it into the score as I am playing it," in real time he has to anticipate what John wants. "I have to be one step ahead of John, but at the same time, be 'on the same page' with him in case he goes in another direction from what I am thinking. It's important that what John is intending comes across to the singers, and that he and I don't contradict each other.

"Sometimes that means playing with a certain articulation to bring something out to the choir. Sometimes it means playing and supporting the choir, but doing it in such a way that John can still hear easily your parts and what is going on in the group." So while we're just learning a piece, Tony is listening carefully to all our voices, finding where we're struggling, and then highlighting that section. On the fly. I remembered noticing one night how Tony played a particularly difficult soprano entrance loudly, and being grateful. I never stopped to think that he is doing that all the time. Seconds later I'd forgotten him again.

Camaraderie wasn't the only sacrifice Tony had to make, he also had to give up some of the music. During rehearsals Tony plays what are called orchestra reductions. "In an orchestra reduction," Tony explains, "the orchestra parts have been arranged down to be played all on the piano, and they are only intended to be used in rehearsal to give the choir a sense of what the orchestra part will sound like." They're usually not written by the composer, and "They're clunky and uncomfortable to play," unlike the piano parts he plays for recitals, which are generally written by the composer and are therefore "much more, as we say, pianistic." At recitals Tony gets to experience the combined joy we feel when we're singing in quartets. It's just him and a singer or another instrumentalist, thrumming together in a "wonderful collaboration," just as we do every Tuesday.

Tony's favorite night of every semester is the dress rehearsal. "I sit out in the house to listen for balance between the choir, soloists, and orchestra. I get to hear the whole piece as intended, with orchestra, soloists, in the space, etc. It's like you're all doing the concert just for me!" And then there are the nights when Tony gets to conduct. "I love being in front of you all, because the energy coming from you is always electric."

Tony conducted Lauridsen's "O Magnum Mysterium" for our 2008 holiday concert. Holiday concerts are, not surprisingly, joyous occasions, but 2008 was particularly jubilant. Barack Obama had been elected president. The relief many of us felt was immense. A friend described how a happily drunken college kid had come up to her and put his arms around her, sobbing, "We did it." A lot of people in New York and around the country and the world exploded with elation that night. I never went to sleep. I stayed up throughout the night with the TV on in the background while constantly checking web pages and blogs and every form of instant communication I could find. I didn't want to miss one second or one expression of celebration.

That particular holiday season was not the happiest time

for soprano Kaarin von Herrlich, however. Three weeks before the concert her fourteen-year-old pit bull–Lab mix Jadie
starting seizing. Although Kaarin rushed her to the hospital,
the doctors were unable to save her. Jadie died. Kaarin was, of
course, devastated. "She was like my firstborn," she lamented.

Thirteen years earlier, Kaarin had opened a bar downtown. At the same time that she was thinking a dog might be
good to have around when she closed up at night alone, Jadie
had been found living by herself in an abandoned building.
Kaarin needed protection, Jadie needed a home. But when
a friend brought Jadie to the bar, Kaarin admitted, "I was
a little afraid of her at first." Kaarin also had two cats at the
time. But she took Jadie home to try it out. "Jadie was fine
with the cats, so I kept her."

From that day on Jadie was always by her side. "She came
to work with me every day, she came on vacation with me. At
home, she would sit next to me on the sofa and gently growl
(moan? talk?) until I petted her. After my daughter was born,
she would lie in the bed at my daughter's feet. Jadie was very
vocal. She would yell for cookies, and she could be very annoying, but not to me. She had a low, quiet bark and it didn't
bother me and it never woke my little girl. She was so loving and intense. I had a lot of friends who were afraid of pit
bulls until they met Jadie. It felt like I lost a part of me when
she died."

We had no idea how much Kaarin was hurting when we
stood beside her at the concert. She'd only told a few people

that her dog had died, and even to those people she hadn't said much. "I wasn't willing or able to admit how completely devastated I was." As we sang one festive piece after another, Kaarin was alone with her sorrow. Until we came to the Lauridsen "O Magnum Mysterium." "It was the line *ut animalia viderent Dominum Natum* (where the text acknowledges that animals were among the first to see the newborn Lord). "We sang it just weeks after Jadie died. It's just so beautiful and loving that animals are included in this mystery. I know it may be written to show how lowly the birth was, but in a way, doesn't it show how exalted the animals were? That they were present and in the presence of this great mystery? And certainly, the way Lauridsen puts it, with such beautiful emphasis on the words *ut animalia*—how soaring, how pretty—I know that's how he means it."

I went back and looked at how Lauridsen had written that section. Kaarin was right. On the words *ut animalia* the sopranos sing higher and higher, and then we stay there, reveling in the word. I also noticed for the first time that we sing the exact same notes on the words *et admirable,* which mean "and wonderful." "O Magnum Mysterium" was one of the most carefully written pieces in Lauridsen's life. "I spent weeks and weeks and weeks, revising and revising, getting it exactly right," Lauridsen told me. There is not a single gratuitous element. It's as simple and spare as the painting that inspired him. If he gave us the same notes for both "and wonderful" and "that animals," it is not an accident. He is making a deliberate musical connection. Kaarin sang those words and in an instant she was no longer alone.

All those days, hours, and weeks Lauridsen had spent holed up in his simple cabin, giving everything he had in order to create music of such extraordinary tenderness it would transcend even the worst suffering, had successfully reached out across years and thousands of miles to a woman he would likely never meet. For the first time that night Kaarin's heart could rest, comforted in a musical embrace of pure understanding. "There is something so sweet about so many voices singing something so personal together," Kaarin told me.

Christina Davis also had a story involving the Lauridsen piece. Two years before, "When my father was dying of pancreatic cancer in 2006, I made him an iPod mix that would allow him to sleep. He had raised me on classical music, encouraged me and my brother to sing in a children's choir, and he had attended every concert that the Choral Society of Grace Church ever gave during my membership. He had been particularly moved by 'O Magnum Mysterium,' and so I chose that song to initiate the compendium of songs. I would watch him turn it on late at night, on the cancer ward, where during his dying he had something like twelve different roommates (noisy, suffering, sleepless) and I knew that that music was being sent through his body as surely as the IV was. And it gave me the only peace I really knew at that time."

When I asked Lauridsen how it felt to create something that has such an effect on people, he said he'd been given a gift. "It's terribly rewarding. I'm completely knocked out by people who come to me and tell me how this has affected their lives. . . . I am a very, very fortunate man."

Ye Shall Have a Song

From Randall Thompson's The Peaceable Kingdom,
written in 1936

**Performed by the Choral Society of Grace Church
in the Winter, 2011**

Water Night

Eric Whitacre, 1995

Performed by Stacy Horn alone on January 10, 2012

Fate and Faith Songs

Britlin Losee, 2011

**Performed by the Women's Choir of the Aaron Copland
School of Music, 2012**

It was the worst heat wave of the summer, and I was once
again walking along Eleventh Street toward Grace Church.
I wasn't heading for rehearsals this time; those wouldn't start
up again until September. I was on my way to feed a friend's

cat. The temperature was up to 104 and the city was retaining heat like an oven. Heat pounded down from the sky while simultaneously radiating up from the streets and out from the brick walls of the building lining the streets. If it didn't mean leaving the poor cat to starve, I wouldn't have gone out. So I trudged onward through the all-encompassing waves, barely taking in my surroundings, just doing my best to keep moving ahead step by step, block by block. Everyone I passed was silent under the weight of the rising temperature, but as soon as I was sure they were out of earshot, I started singing. John had just e-mailed the selections for our December concert program, and among them was Randall Thompson's *Peaceable Kingdom*. At the end of *The Peaceable Kingdom* is the most hopeful line I have ever sung in my life. Although the text is from the Bible, I don't have to transpose the meaning to fit my beliefs and outlook; the words fit every ideology. I could barely breathe, but out they came: Ye shall have a song and gladness of heart.

I would have sounded like a crazy person to anyone who heard me. Not because I was singing in that life-draining heat, but because watching someone sing a choral piece alone is like seeing someone have a lively conversation with not just one imaginary person but a whole crowd of them. It starts off okay, you sing your part, but then you have to keep pausing while you listen in your head to what all the other parts are doing. Sing-pause-sing-pause-pause-sing. You can try singing all the voice parts, but then you wouldn't be the person with an imaginary crowd, you'd be the person who thought she *was* the imaginary crowd. The Sybil of song. I went with pausing.

The city was slowly roasting me alive, but I was happily, weirdly singing away until I came to my favorite part of the chorus, and then I stopped. All the different voice parts had been repeatedly singing the words "goeth with a pipe," and along with all the sopranos in my head, I was about to hit the stratosphere, to thrill with a ravishing high A for four whole measures, when it hit me. The last time I sang this piece I was a soprano 1. Was that a soprano 1 line? I couldn't remember. I tried to think through the entire piece. If there were four voice parts (soprano, tenor, alto, bass) I was safe. That meant all the sopranos sang the same line and I would get to sing that high A. If there were eight, that meant the sopranos broke up into soprano 1 and 2 and I would be singing something else. But the voices in my head were too vague. I wouldn't know for sure until I could go home and check the score.

The next couple of hours were torture. I still had to walk all the way across town in the heat, which I was now miserably aware of with each step. Then I had to feed the cat, spend some time with it, feed the fish, water the plants, pet the cat some more, and then make my way back west. Wait, wait, wait, more horrible heat, wait, wait, wait, then home.

When I finally got back to my apartment, I ripped through my pile of music, found *The Peaceable Kingdom* score, opened it up, and at first I rejoiced. *Four parts.* I was so relieved I flipped to "Ye Shall Have a Song," which I intended to sing in celebration, when I learned the awful truth. Roughly half the pieces in the score were broken into eight parts and of course "Ye Shall Have a Song" was one of them.

I tried to keep an open mind. Maybe the soprano 2 part was every bit as rapturous as the soprano 1. This has been the case in every soprano 2 part I've sung so far. Maybe I wouldn't get that high A moment, but I'd get a different high A moment. I sang through the soprano 2 line. Compared to the emotional heights reached in the soprano 1, it felt sluggish and subdued.

There was one more chance for musical redemption. The true test would be singing the soprano 2 line with the other parts. What is not so beautiful alone might be glorious when put together with other voices. I wouldn't know for sure until I had sung it with the rest of the choir. And that meant I wouldn't know until September.

It was a long, depressing summer. I'd been going through my posts on Echo (an online service, aka social network, that I started in 1990) when I came across one I'd written exactly five years before, when I was about to turn fifty:

"I just had a horrible thought. I don't want to turn fifty and still be alone. Like a dog. As it were. But seriously. I freaking do not want that to happen."

It happened. Five years later and I'm still alone. I went to a summer sing to cheer myself up about my newly found heights of loserdom, but after the first chorus a woman in front of me turned around, pointed to my friend Barbara, who was sitting next to me, and said to her friend, "She's good." Not "they're good." "*She's* good." For the rest of the night I was sure I was flat.

The next sing I went to was huge, and the whoops and cheers at the beginning started to bring back the tiniest glimmer of hope. It's one measly high A, I told myself. It's hardly the end of the world, and okay, the whole being alone-like-a-dog thing sucks, but that could still change. The first conductor of the night got up and, before launching into the very first piece of the night, said, "Express yourself, enjoy yourself, control yourself." Yeah . . . no. *I want that high A. Damnit.*

In the middle of the summer John e-mailed our part assignments. He doesn't change parts often, so I was already planning on how I'd cheer myself up—two slices of pizza for dinner, new shoes, a pedicure; maybe even more drastic measures, like a puppy—when I saw a one next to my name. I was a soprano 1 again. I'd later learn that he assigned everyone based on which part they sang the last time we performed the piece, but in that moment it was a tiny miracle. It opened the door to larger-miracle-possibility ahead.

On the first night of rehearsal we each received a great big book of music. Pages one through twenty-eight weren't even music, but instructions about score markings, dynamics, discipline, counting, diction, articulation, and vowel and consonant pronunciation in Latin, Italian, French, and German. John once again introduced all the new people and as usual I looked in vain for a new man in my age range. It was a fun evening in spite of the no-new-men disappointment, and I was dying to sing "Ye Shall Have a Song," but we didn't get to it that night. On my way home, though, it came up on my iPod. I ran into a neighbor when I walked into my building. He looked at me in my headphones and said, "We should have a day where everyone unplugs from everything and talks." I agreed with him, but at the top of the stairs I thought, "We should unplug and sing." Then, remembering Eric Whitacre's TED talk about his Virtual Choir, I thought of one more variation: We could plug in and sing.

After joining the Virtual Choir mailing list, I didn't hear anything for the longest time. Every once in a while Whitacre would tweet that they were almost ready, but he never gave any details. That was fine with me. It wasn't as if I was going to participate.

Rehearsals for our holiday concerts continued, and for the next few months I had the pleasure of singing "Ye Shall Have a Song" and hitting that high A repeatedly. Then concert week arrived. We had three holiday performances that year, which meant I had three opportunities to sing "Ye Shall Have a Song." By the third night, when we got to that section of the program, I was sobbing so hard I had trouble reading my music and I almost missed my beloved high A. It was the line "Ye shall have a song, and gladness of heart," and in particular the "gladness of heart" part. What more could anyone want or ask of life than gladness of heart? Such a simple thing. And I was to have it, the text promised. All that possibility dangling in front of me, carried in music so irresistible that my heart had no choice but to open. But even as hope welled within me, a part of me worried that I was being beguiled into believing and that disappointment would inevitably follow.

I looked around the church, which was radiant through my tears. What had changed so much since that night long ago when I was a teenager and sang for the first time in a church during the holidays? There were smiling faces now as there were then, and flashes of gold, red, and green, and this time there were also pine trees and a cerulean blue ceiling spread with stars. Like the first time, the whole church was alive with good cheer and here I was, still fighting tears. But back then my whole life was in front of me and I was bursting with gladness of heart. Now I couldn't say with complete confidence that my heart was glad or that I even believed it ever would be again. I mean, maybe it was and maybe I did. I couldn't decide. Isn't this something one should know? And so I cried. The next morning I put my music away and waited for rehearsals to resume in January.

A couple of weeks later, on December 21, at 9:36 a.m., an e-mail arrived announcing that everything was ready to go for Virtual Choir 3. This time the choir would be singing Whitacre's "Water Night," an a cappella chorus he wrote in forty-five minutes in 1995, when he was twenty-five years old. *Oh for the love of god. Are composers even human?* The deadline for submission was January 31, 2012. It wasn't a lot of time. People making videos for the Virtual Choir 2 had three and a half months. This time they had five weeks.

Within a half hour of the announcement, the servers hosting Whitacre's website crashed. The response was enormous. People from twenty countries had signed up, and every day the numbers climbed. Until that e-mail arrived I hadn't committed to participating. But once I read the announcement I realized that I had actually known all along that there was no way in the world I would miss this. I ordered a copy of the score for "Water Night" and started practicing.

I'd made up my mind to do this, but the process was terrifying. Everyone submits videos of themselves singing their voice part, and all the submissions are later stitched together into a choir. There is no selection process. Everyone who submits a video is included. But when you submit your video you're not one voice of many, there is only you. Exposed. Eric Whitacre and whoever is on his team will be able to hear every note, every mistake, every poorly timed breath.

In addition to what I sounded like in my video submission, I had one other concern, and this one made me even more anxious: what I looked like. I started shooting videos of myself singing. I tried versions with glasses on, glasses off, hair pulled back, hair down. I experimented with different webcam angles (I was working with the built-in camera in my computer). Sometimes I sat close to the screen, sometimes farther away. After carefully studying all the results, I went with glasses on, hair down, and sitting close to the screen, which was positioned a little above me so that I was looking slightly up, my most flattering angle.

Once I felt comfortable with the soprano 1 part, I put my headphones on and recorded myself singing along with the "Water Night" recording on Eric Whitacre's web page. There was nothing in "Water Night" even approaching the complicated and fiendishly tricky runs I was currently working on for the Choral Society's next piece, the Verdi *Requiem,* so I was feeling relatively calm and confident. When I was done, I sat back with my coffee and listened. In all the sustained sections, whenever the music went *forte* and I couldn't hear myself singing, I went flat. When I sang the highest note in the piece, an A-flat, I screeched. All throughout the recording my voice sounded weak and squeaky, and I took breaths constantly. At the end, when we had to hold our last note for four measures, or sixteen beats, which Whitacre slowed down and extended, I couldn't do it. I was left with my mouth open, no sound emerging, musically impotent.

And there it was. I'd always known I wasn't a great singer, but what I didn't know was that I was truly bad. From beginning to end, I sounded terrible. There wasn't a single pretty or even acceptable moment in my entire recording. It hit me that I'd spent the past thirty years doing something I loved that I couldn't, in fact, do. I couldn't participate in the Virtual Choir now. I wasn't going to put this up there for all the world and Eric Whitacre to see, not to mention John Maclay and everyone in my choir. And how could I go back to the Choral Society now that I'd discovered how poorly I sang?

I felt like I'd just lost 152 best friends. I immediately went to the Virtual Choir 3 page on Facebook. I didn't know where else to go. I was feeling awful and I wanted that feeling to stop. I had this vague idea that I'd find people there like myself, singers who'd made recordings and realized they couldn't sing, either, and then I wouldn't feel so alone.

The first thing I saw when I got there was a picture of a heavily marked-up page from the "Water Night" score, which had been posted by an alto named Kristen Soo. Kristen wanted to know if other singers wrote in their scores like she did. I clicked on the picture. In one section she wrote, "epic alto harmony." I laughed. It was like my practice of putting asterisks over my favorite parts. Then I saw something written over the exact same measures where I had gone horribly flat: "keep pitch." Which meant Kristen Soo had gone flat there, as well. In the next few seconds I couldn't type fast enough. I posted about how happy I was to read that she'd gone flat in the same spot, and within minutes all these other singers posted that they'd had trouble there, too. Common problem. No big deal. "Yeah, you gotta watch yourself there." I went from feeling like I'd lost 152 friends to gaining thousands. Kristen Soo's JPEG had saved my musical life.

I tried again. My problem was going flat whenever I couldn't hear myself and that particular section is marked *forte*. This time I focused very intensely. I couldn't hear myself sing, but

I could feel it, and I concentrated on keeping the feeling the same. I didn't go flat. I couldn't believe that was all it took. Trying harder. I went back to work on the piece in earnest.

My plan was to practice right up until the deadline, but then I remembered that I'd finally made a date to begin getting the dental work I needed, and my dentist had warned me that it might temporarily affect my speech and singing.

On January 10, I washed and blow dried my hair, put on lipstick, glasses, and the dark top we'd been instructed to wear, and started warming up my voice. The submission process had changed a little for Virtual Choir 3. This time, instead of making the video yourself and uploading it to YouTube, singers went to the Virtual Choir web page and recorded their submissions there. You put on headphones, and then you had to choose Practice or Record. If you chose Record, whatever you sang was saved, and you could record as many versions as you liked, deleting all but the best one when you were done. I'd been practicing for weeks, so I hit Record.

A video of Eric Whitacre appeared. The simple black T-shirt he wore when the Virtual Choir sang *Lux Aurumque* had been replaced with a well-tailored and elegant black suit. He looked stunning. (I've since learned that he has signed with Storm Models in London.) Whitacre looked directly into the camera, which made it appear as if he was staring straight at you, and that was a little unnerving at first. Being conducted normally doesn't feel so one-on-one. Whitacre and I clapped together three times to sync our timing, then a piano sounded out the opening notes, Eric raised his hands, and on the downbeat the choir in my headphones and I began.

I'd decided ahead of time that if I lost my confidence about maintaining pitch in the *forte* sections, I'd turn the sound down. If there was any danger of not making that high A-flat, I'd switch to the soprano 2 part. Cheating of this sort was encouraged. If you can't make a note, don't sing it, we were told. Whatever you had to do was allowed.

I watched Whitacre do his best to conduct a choir he could neither see nor hear, and I did my best to follow him. Occasionally he'd close his eyes and assume a blissful expression in response to whatever he was hearing, which I knew couldn't be me or any other virtual choir singer. He had no way of knowing if I was accurately interpreting his gestures, and I had no way of knowing if I was giving him what he wanted. But maybe—if we both managed to occupy that space that musicians strive to reach—in those few minutes we each knew what the other was feeling. "My music is hyperautobiographical," Whitacre told me in a phone interview. "There's no separation between my music and my personality. It's the same thing. When my music is out there I feel it's me connecting and communicating with people the same way I would if we were together in a room and just speaking."

I sang as carefully and as well as I could. While there might not be anything in "Water Night" as challenging as the Verdi fugue I was currently struggling with, it is difficult in other ways. Like most of Whitacre's compositions, "Water Night" is filled with dissonant chords that are held, or suspended; and as they slowly progress and resolve and then suspend again (sometimes resolving and suspending at the same time), different harmonies emerge, creating an effect that is the vocal equivalent of shimmering. It works only as long as everyone holds his or her note absolutely steady. However, staying on your note when there are sometimes up to fourteen different voice parts around you singing what sounds, at first, just plain wrong, takes practice. But it is precisely those sections that are the most satisfying to sing. To "sit there for a second fully preparing for the next phrase," soprano Chrystina Gastelum wrote me, "just feeling the vibration of that dissonance linger . . . some of the resolutions are just decadent." "There definitely is a physical sensation," Karen Arneson said. "It feels like a ringing in your body, which feels spiritual to me." She is not alone. "Whitacre has a gift for stirring the soul with his music and the experience never dulls," Roland Jarquio said. "I feel the same way each time." I wanted the thrill of that quiet tremor. So I focused on keeping my notes simple and pure. No vibrato, no wavering of pitch. (I hoped.)

I played back my first try. I hadn't gone flat in the sustained sections. I went flat in whole new sections. My breathing problems remained, and in spite of all my effort to look nice I looked old, tense, and miserable. This was not fun. I felt as though all the technology currently at our command was being used to make an already vulnerable act that much more traumatic. The payback of singing in a choir—the corresponding joy of singing with other people—is completely absent in the Virtual Choir experience. No one stood beside me as I sang. My voice would eventually join with others, but I wouldn't be there when it happened.

When I first saw Eric Whitacre's TED talk, my reaction was, Why wouldn't everyone in the world want to do this? Now I was thinking, Why in the world would anyone want to do this? Eric Whitacre himself wouldn't do it. "I made seven or eight attempts to join the last Virtual Choir," he told me in a Skype interview, "and I threw them all away. I said no way I'm putting this out there. It's hard."

But I'd come this far, and I couldn't give up now. I'd seen the final result of Virtual Choir 1 and Virtual Choir 2. I knew how amazing it was going to be in the end. I wanted my voice joined with the others in that future shimmer. I kept recording and deleting what I'd recorded until I made a version I could live with. Then I made one more just for fun, and that is the one I ultimately used. It wasn't great, either, but overall my voice and tone were more relaxed and (more important) I looked better.

The first thing I did after submitting my video was run back to the Virtual Choir page on Facebook. I was surging with that sense of invincibility you get whenever you have done something you were terrified to do. My heart was finally, incontrovertibly, emphatically, glad. I didn't want to let that feeling go. I knew there were all these other Virtual Choir singers out there whose hearts must be racing, too, and this is where I'd find them. "I submitted my video!" I posted. Almost instantaneously, a string of congratulations and "likes" appeared. I stayed on that page and kept the postsinging high going as long as I could. I also tweeted about it and blogged about it. I posted on Echo about it. In short, I wallowed.

"These souls all on their own desert island . . . sending electronic messages in bottles to each other," Whitacre has said of his virtual singers. From a recent BBC interview: "People simply want to connect and they will do anything to connect with each other, and the technology really is secondary. What they're doing is sitting alone in their room and there is a shared intention, a global shared intention. They know that somehow they'll sing alone, their video will be uploaded and they'll be connected to all these other people, and it truly creates this virtual family."

But there are much, much easier ways to virtually connect. Millions of them. What makes people brave such a terrifying, potentially publicly embarrassing process in order to participate in this choir? Almost everyone I contacted told me they were moved to tears by Virtual Choirs 1 and 2. Lynna Schaefer in Albany, New York, said, "I decided to listen to my tears, essentially." Jenny Smith Mayes in Sydney, Australia, wrote, "There was no way the Jenny I knew would EVER put herself out there in the World Wide Web for all to see and hear, but the urge to be part of this community and be connected in a world that seemed to be falling apart was overwhelming." Bren Norris in Sonoma, California, sang even though she'd had a diving accident at age sixty that made it impossible for her to hold long notes. "In fact, in one recording I was at the end and started coughing and couldn't stop. I had to re-record." She persevered because she'd fallen in love with Whitacre's music and "I just had to be a part of it." When she was done, Jenny from Australia was so excited, "I ran around my living room squealing like a school girl. After calming down though, I stayed on the Virtual Choir Facebook page. I was not ready to sever my connection just yet." Bren added, "What he is doing in the world is bigger than his music."

In his book *A Philosophy of Music Education,* Bennett Reimer, the former chair of the Music Education Department at Northwestern University, wrote about performing, "The power of such experience is so great and its satisfactions so deep that those who have shared it are likely to be changed fundamentally in their relation to music. For such people music inevitably becomes a source of some of life's deepest rewards. This is no small matter, given the universal need for such satisfaction and its rarity in human life."

For almost three decades the National Endowment for the Arts has been measuring participation in the arts, and in 2011 they announced that they would begin to "measure and analyze a fuller spectrum of artistic genres, arts participation via electronic media, and personal arts creation." What they've found so far is that "nearly 75 percent of adults attended arts activities, created art, or engaged with art via electronic media." This was more than twice the percentage of adults who went in person to concerts, plays, the ballet, or museums. And of all the art forms people were involved with via the Internet and other mobile devices, classical music was the one they were engaging with the most.

In the last few days before the Virtual Choir 3 deadline, I watched submissions soar. On the morning of January 30, the number of video entries was up to around 1,700. The next morning it was 2,300. On the final day of submissions the servers were so overwhelmed that once again they crashed. Over on Facebook, the people providing technical assistance to singers were giving out so much advice, Facebook disabled commenting on their accounts, and the helpers were forced to quickly create new identities. Whitacre extended the deadline twenty-four hours. In the end there were 3,746 submissions from 2,945 people in 73 countries.

As the Virtual Choir evolved and grew, Britlin Losee, the young soprano who inspired Eric Whitacre to create the choir, graduated high school, started college, and inspired by Whitacre's music, became a composer herself. In 2012 Britlin took the stage at the Aaron Copland School of Music in New York and conducted her choral piece, *Fate and Faith Songs*. I watched a video of the event on YouTube. Her energy and movements as she crosses the stage and readies herself are as quick and excited as a baby bird's. Then the music begins, slow, quiet, and haunting. In the first movement, the lyrics (her own) describe love as "an illusion," but when the women lament, "you've pulled apart my web of stars" the music has a strangely harmonious combination of darkness and joy. It reminds me of the composer Tomás Luis de Victoria, whose compositions always managed to sound happy even when he was writing about something sad. By now I shouldn't be surprised by the depth and accomplishment in one so young, but it still takes me aback. In the sunnier second movement, when the women sing of "smiling with kisses that awaken us to life," the harmonies are lovely, bright and sparkling. I played the video again and again.

Before she discovered Whitacre's music, Britlin had never thought of herself as a serious composer. But once she heard "Sleep," she told me in a telephone interview, "That was it for me." Her first response was to reach out to the man responsible for focusing her direction in life. "I was trying to figure out how I could contact him, where it would be more likely that he would be able to hear what I had to say." She knew he must get inundated with e-mail. That's when she came up with the idea of posting a video of herself singing. "A video would stand out."

The most she hoped for in response was a simple acknowledgment that he'd seen it. Perhaps someday she'd get his autograph. Hours later, however, she came back to the following message on her Facebook wall:

> This was absolutely beautiful. I'm so humbled and honored
> by your kind words and your clear voice. I listened to your

composition as well, and have no doubt that you are well on your way to becoming an exceptional and completely original artist. Now I can say "I knew you when." ;-)

I wonder if you would be brave enough to put this video on Vimeo, or Youtube, and let me blog about it. . . . It just gave me the most incredible idea, and I'd like to use your video as a "test" to show other singers what is possible. What do you think?

Again, THANK YOU, and keep up all the incredible work. Your passion and dedication to music will take you wherever you'd like to go.

Warmest regards,
Eric Whitacre

Back at her computer, Britlin was running around her bedroom screaming. "Thank you soooooooooooooooo much for listening to everything and thank you for what you've said here!" she posted back. "Thank you so much. You don't know how happy I am right now . . . Yes!!! . . . Thank you so much for all that you said about my voice and compositions. You are amazing!!!! I love your work and you as a person!!! Thank you!!!!!!!"

A month later, at Whitacre's invitation, Britlin and her family attended a performance of Whitacre's music at Lincoln Center. After the concert Britlin and her parents went to the green room to meet him. Whitacre's eyes widened when he spotted Britlin and he immediately came over and put his arms around her.

When I interviewed Whitacre, he spoke about his "first and biggest influence," Morten Lauridsen. He told me how Lauridsen had approached him after a 1992 performance of Whitacre's music, when Whitacre was twenty-two. "Even then he was a godlike figure among choral singers," Whitacre said, "and he had this aura. . . . He looks like Brahms." Lauridsen introduced himself and invited Whitacre to lunch. "To this day I use him as an example for what I'd like to be to young composers and young artists. He was unbelievably open, very supportive, we talked a lot about composing but he never lectured to me. It couldn't have been a more gracious way to invite me into the coven of composers and I'm forever grateful to him for that."

Britlin Losee is twenty-one years old now. "Anytime I've seen him," she wrote me about Whitacre, "he's always looked at me with thankful eyes. At the Paley Center Virtual Choir 2 premiere last year, before the show even started, he came up to me in the first row and bent a knee to talk with me."

In the months since I listened to Britlin's choral piece, she's kept working. She's written a piano piece dedicated to our soldiers called "Bellator Somnium" (The Warrior's Dream) and a choral composition for men's and women's voices titled "The Silver Lining." When her professor listened to the second piece he was speechless. There was nothing really to be said except who would perform it and when (the Queens College Choir in the fall). The young girl who inspired such an amazing thing is growing up and creating amazing and inspiring things herself.

I AM NOT a great singer. Luckily, though, not being the greatest singer in the world may work in my favor. According to the study titled "Does singing promote well-being?" the amateurs in the study experienced a heightened sense of joy and well-being following singing lessons. The professionals did not. "Amateurs don't have the hang-ups of full-on professionals," our associate conductor Tony Bellomy wrote me. "It is easy for professionals, me included, to get wrapped up in music as a job. This will kill the music faster than anything. Serious amateurs never seem to cross that line. It's because they are participating in music purely out of love for it."

The authors of the study "Effects of Group Singing and Performance for Marginalized and Middle-Class Singers" bluntly but reassuringly stated that "group singing and performance can produce satisfying and therapeutic sensations even when the sound produced by the vocal instrument is of mediocre quality."

Gareth Malone, a British conductor, has made a living out of turning people who would never think of themselves as singers into choirs. His efforts can be seen in the BBC reality TV series *The Choir*. Last season he put together a choir made up of military wives whose husbands were fighting in Afghanistan. I watched the first episode. I have never seen women so determined *not* to sing. It took all of Malone's coaxing skills to bring enough of them to the choral table to make a choir. Not long after, they recorded a single titled "Wherever You Are." The text came from letters between the wives and their husbands, which composer Paul Mealor then set to music. When the song became the U.K.'s best-selling Christmas single that year, Mealor said, "Music has to be useful and shouldn't exist in an ivory tower," pointing out that "Mozart's music was sung in the street."

"It makes little difference whether the singing society be a proud metropolitan organization which piles up its hundreds of singers in terraces for the annual Christmas-tide production of *The Messiah,* or a country choir that looks up to *Sound the Loud Timbrel* as the pinnacle of its wildest ambition," wrote nineteenth-century music critic Henry E. Krehbiel, "the influence which it sends through its community, like currents from so many galvanic batteries, is the most potent and healthful medium which the art of music has." If they'd had virtual choirs then, he would have included them, too.

"The wonderful thing about concert week," John e-mailed us, "is that people of varying strengths and levels of preparation all get to the finish line together." Regardless of my own assessment of my singing abilities, I get to stand near some of the loveliest voices I've ever heard, as well as those of people who are struggling, and to be a part of the glorious amalgamation that always seems to work.

"I believe that all the arts, and especially music, are necessary to a full life," Ralph Vaughan Williams said. "Music will show you what to do with your life." I'll take it even further. Music, this choir, in some ways is my life. We all need a way off the couch or the floor; a way to embrace the fall or whatever else life brings. When I joined the choir I was only looking to soothe a broken heart. Instead I found something that invariably transcends every misfortune I've faced and makes me happy. Every week, music dependably and effectively silences my roulette wheel of worry and self-doubt, and that is not a small thing. Nor is it the only thing.

"When I think about who my closest friends are," my fellow soprano Lucia Rivieccio told me, "they are all people I've met in choir or met through people in choir . . . just the opportunity to meet so many different kinds of people. It can be a bit of a ragtag group, some people can be really annoying, others I don't know very well but like very much, and some I just adore. But I wouldn't want to lose even one."

"Ordinary human beings can do extraordinary things," John once e-mailed us. "Belief is necessary—not in any one creed or religion, or in religion at all—but belief in yourself and in each other."

I believe. I believe in singing. Like Brian Eno, I believe in singing with other people. I know it won't last forever. "There are people joining the choir now who were born when we first joined," Barbara pointed out to me once. One by one we will all be replaced. But I hope that like Frits Menschaar, the bass in our choir who was singing right up until the week he died, I will be able to continue singing until the very end. "How long do you plan to sing with this or other choral groups," I asked the people in my choir. Nancy Tepper's simple answer summed it up best. "As long as I can."

CODA

Last Tuesday night John asked us to turn to page 64 of the Verdi *Requiem*. I stopped breathing for a second. I knew exactly what was on page 64. It's the final section of the Dies irae, or Day of Wrath, the hymn in the *Requiem* about judgment day, one of my favorite parts. Every Tuesday night I pray for John to ask us to turn to page 64 and I have been diligently practicing for just this moment.

The section begins with the sopranos and the altos singing *Huic ergo parce, Deus.* "Spare him therefore, God." The women are asking for the guilty to be forgiven. Verdi gives us one word of direction: *dolcissimo.* Such a musical, evocative word. Dol-CHESS-imo. You can almost tell what it means just by the sound of it. For the record, it means sing with as much sweetness and tenderness as you can muster. Nothing less than eternity is at stake. The melodies Verdi gives us make it impossible to sing it any other way. But you don't get the full effect until all the different voice parts are singing together.

The sweetness that Verdi wrote to embody such an important request as forgiveness and mercy comes from the harmony. No one voice alone can produce this sound. This was the moment I'd been practicing for.

Rehearsal was in the church that night. It was a little on the dark side, but there was enough light to see. John raised his arms, I looked down at my music, the page covered in my handwritten asterisks, and we began. Voices sparked into life all around me, like matches being lit, but gently, as if someone's hands were slightly covering and protecting the flame. The music we made was as lyrical and angelic as anyone could have hoped. John made a few comments about how we could do it even better and once again raised his arms. I couldn't believe my luck. We were going to sing it again. Once more we intoned the line *Huic ergo parce, Deus.* Because it was John, he had to make sure it was perfect, and he made still more suggestions when we finished. While he concentrated on getting our voices just right, we sang that section over and over, reveling in the warm glow of our voices, and the magic current of potential that comes to life whenever people are drawn together by the astonishing and irresistible power of a song.

SOURCE NOTES

Prelude

Davis, James J. *The Iron Puddler: My Life in the Rolling Mills and What Came of It.* New York: Grosset & Dunlap Publishers, 1922.
———. "The Power of Music." Address before the National Association of Music Merchants. Commodore Hotel, New York, June 7, 1922.
Department of the Interior, Bureau of Mines. Report on Black Blasting Powder Explosion, Baltimore Tunnel No. 2 Mine, Delaware and Hudson Coal Company, Wilkes Barre, Pennsylvania. June 5, 1919.

A German Requiem

Jourdain, Robert. *Music, the Brain, and Ecstasy: How Music Captures Our Imagination.* New York: William Morrow & Co., 1997.
Mussulman, J. A. *Dear People . . . Robert Shaw: A Biography.* Bloomington: Indiana University Press, 1979.
Swafford, Jan. *Johannes Brahms: A Biography.* New York: Random House, 1997.

Kirshnit, Fred. "God Is in the Music." *New York Sun,* December 20, 2005.

Thuleen, Nancy. "Ein deutsches Requiem: (Mis)conceptions of the Mass." Online article, 1998, nthuleen.com/papers/415brahms .html.

Recitative: The Orpheus Glee Club

Interviews with Anthony Brooks, executive director of the Luzerne County Historical Society, and John Lohman, treasurer and historian of the Orpheus Choral Society.

The history of the Orpheus Glee Club was compiled from ten years of articles (March 1, 1919, to July 15, 1929) from *The (Pittsburg, PA) Druid.*

Campbell Bartoletti, Susan. *Growing up in Coal Country.* Boston: Houghton Mifflin Books for Children, 1996.
Husband, Joseph. *A Year in a Coal-Mine.* Boston: Houghton Mifflin Company, 1911.
Miller, Donald L., and R. E. Sharpless. *The Kingdom of Coal.* Philadelphia: University of Pennsylvania Press, 1996.

The (Connellsville, PA) Weekly Courier, June 12, 1919.

Davis, James J. "The Power of Music." Address before the National Association of Music Merchants, Commodore Hotel, New York, June 7, 1922.

Mining deaths: www.msha.gov.

The Chichester Psalms

Interview with Mark Whittle, Ph.D., Department of Astronomy, University of Virginia.

Burton, Humphrey. *Leonard Bernstein*. New York: Doubleday, 1994.
Levitin, Daniel J. *This Is Your Brain on Music*. New York: Penguin Books, 2007.

Curtis, M. E., and J. J. Bharucha. "The minor third communicates sadness in speech, mirroring its use in music." *Emotion*, June, 2010.
Nash, Ethan. "Understanding and Performing Bernstein's Chichester Psalms." *Choral Journal* 49, no. 8, February 2009.
Whittle, Mark. "Primordial Sounds: Big Bang Acoustics." Press release, American Astronomical Society meeting, Denver, June, 2004.

Bohem, Leslie, scriptwriter. *Taken*. TV series, Sci-Fi Channel, 2002.

Recitative: The Rubinstein Club

William Rogers Chapman papers, 1921–1938. JPB 06–27, Music Division, The New York Public Library for the Performing Arts.
Mendelssohn Glee Club Papers. JPB 06–5, Boxes 1, 3, 4, 6, 17–22, 27–30, Music Division, The New York Public Library for the Performing Arts.

Caswell, Mina Holway. *The Ministry of Music: The Life of William Rogers Chapman*. Portland, ME.: The Southworth-Anthoensen Press, 1938.

Krehbiel, Henry Edward. *Review of the New York musical season 1888–1889.* New York & London: Novello, Ewer & Co., 1889.

"Music and Musicians, Some Current Gossip." *New-York Tribune,* December 15, 1887.

"The Doings of Musicians." *New-York Tribune,* June 4, 1888.

"Concert of the Rubinstein Club." *New-York Tribune,* April 18, 1890.

Krehbiel, Henry Edward. "American Choral Societies and Conductors." *Harper's Weekly,* February 1, 1890.

"The Man Who Brought Music to Maine." *Down East,* January 1975.

Messiah

The archives of Grace Church, New York City.

Interviews with Frank Cedric Smith and Patrick J. Allen, D.M.A. (former and current organists and masters of choristers of Grace Church, New York City).

Burrows, Donald. *Messiah.* Cambridge: Cambridge University Press, 1991.

Hale Smith, Matthew. *Sunshine and Shadow in New York.* Hartford, CT: J. B. Burr and Company, 1868; online at Internet Archive Text Archive: www.archive.org/details/sunshine shadowinoosmitrich.

Lord, Walter. *A Night to Remember,* Holt, Rinehart & Winston, 1955.

Melville, Herman. "The Two Temples," in Great Short Works of Herman Melville. ed. Warner Berthoff. New York: Perennial Classics, HarperCollins, 2004.

Ogasapian, John. *Church Music in America*. Chamblee, GA: Mercer University Press, 2007.

Rhinelander Stewart, William. *Grace Church and Old New York*. New York: E. P. Dutton & Company, 1924.

Carmer, Carl. "The Years of Grace: 1808–1958." New York: Grace Church, 1958.

Foley, Barbara. "From Wall Street to Astor Place: Historicizing Melville's 'Bartleby.' " *American Literature* 72, no. 1, 2000.

Knowles, Art. "Edith Corse Evans and the Titanic Disaster." *The Titanic Commutator* 33, no. 187, 2009.

Kandell, Jonathan. "The Glorious History of Handel's Messiah: A musical rite of the holiday season, the Baroque-era oratorio still awes listeners 250 years after the composer's death." *Smithsonian Magazine*, December 2009.

Salon, Michael. "A Study of Worship, Music and Musicians at Three Churches in Greenwich Village." Degree project, Yale Institute of Sacred Music, April 1, 1986.

The New York Times. "They Don't Like Chants." January 5, 1893.

———. "Grace Church Music." January 6, 1893.

E. Bunting [organist and choirmaster, Greenburg Presbyterian Church]. Letter to the editor. *The New York Times*, January 13, 1913.

Letter from Rev. Benjamin Minifie to Frank Cedric Smith, June 21, 1960.

"The Church Music for 1893–94." A Pastoral Letter To the People of Grace Church. March 20, 1893.

"The Ministry of Music." Friends of Grace Church Music Newsletter, vol. 1, no. 1, March, 1977.

Toward the Unknown Region

Cooke, Nym. "Sacred music to 1800"; and Preston, Katherine K. "Art music from 1800 to 1860." in *The Cambridge History of American Music.* Edited by David Nicholls. Cambridge: Cambridge University Press, 1998.

Garretson Robert L. *Choral Music: History, Style, and Performance Practice.* Saddle River, NJ: Prentice Hall, 1993.

Gay, Peter. *Mozart.* New York: Penguin Lives/Viking, 1999.

Jacobs, Arthur, ed. *Choral Music: A Symposium.* London, New York: Pelican Books, 1966.

Kennedy, Michael. *The Works of Ralph Vaughan Williams.* Cambridge: Oxford University Press, 1964.

Maitland, Ermengard. *F. W. Maitland: A Child's-Eye View.* London: Bernard Quaritch (for the Selden Society), 1957.

Poultney, David. *Studying Music History: Learning, Reason, and Writing About Music History and Literature.* Saddle River, NJ: Prentice Hall, 1983.

Robinson, Ray, ed., *Choral Music: A Norton Historical Anthology.* New York: W. W. Norton & Company, 1978.

Steinberg, Michael. *Choral Masterworks: A Listener's Guide.* New York: Oxford University Press, 2005.

Summer, Robert J. *Choral Masterworks from Back to Britten: Reflections of a Conductor.* Metuchen, NJ: The Scarecrow Press, 2007.

Vaughan Williams, Ralph. *National Music and Other Essays.* London: Oxford University Press 1934.

Vaughan Williams, Ursula. *RVW: A Biography of Ralph Vaughan Williams.* Oxford: Oxford University Press, 1964.

Young, Percy M. *The Choral Tradition*. New York: W. W. Norton & Company, 1971.

Crook, David. "A Sixteenth Century Catalogue of Prohibited Music." *Journal of the American Musicological Society* 62, no. 1, Spring 2009.

Krehbiel, Henry Edward. "American Choral Societies and Conductors." *Harper's Weekly*, February 1, 1890.

Heffer, Simon. "Why Ralph Vaughan Williams should be as revered as Shakespeare." *The (London) Telegraph*, August 20, 2008.

Recitative: The People's Choral Union

New York County Court of General Sessions, indictment files, 1892. Available at Municipal Archives of the City of New York, Damrosch—Tee Van Collection, 1856–1969, Library of Congress; and Frank Damrosch Papers, JPB 88-25, Music Division, The New York Public Library for the Performing Arts.

Cohen, Julius. *They Builded Better Than They Knew*. New York: Julian Messner, 1971.

Olmstead, Andrea. *Julliard: A History*. Champagne: University of Illinois Press, 1999.

Stebbins, Lucy Poate. *Frank Damrosch: Let the People Sing*. Durham, NC: Duke University Press, 1945

"Admirer of the P.C.U." Letter to the editor. *The New York Times*, January 18, 1902.

"Love of Music Growing." *The Washington Post*, April 8, 1906.

Mass No. 11 in D Minor, *aka* Missa in Angustiis

Heartz, Daniel. *Mozart, Haydn and Early Beethoven: 1781–1802.* New York: W. W. Norton & Company, 2009.

Jourdain, Robert. *Music, the Brain, and Ecstasy: How Music Captures Our Imagination.* New York: William Morrow & Co., 1997.

Klein, Hermann. *Unmusical New York: A Brief Criticism of Triumphs, Failures, and Abuses.* London, New York: John Lane, 1910; New York: Da Capo Press, 1979.

Lampadius, Wilhelm Adolf. *Life of Felix Mendelssohn.* New York & Philadelphia: F. Leypoldt, 1865.

Wyn Jones, David, ed. Haydn. Oxford Composer Companions. New York: Oxford University Press, 2002.

Chorus America. "How Children, Adults, and Communities Benefit from Choruses." The Chorus Impact Study, 2009.

Bell, Cindy L. "Toward a definition of a community choir." International Journal of Community Music 1, no. 2, 2008.

Harrer, Gerhart. *Grundlagen der Musiktherapie und Musikpsychologie.* Stuttgart: Gustav Fischer Verlag, 1975.

Whitacre, Eric. "A virtual choir 2,000 voices strong." TEDTalk, ted.com/talks, March 2011.

Ave Maria

Interview with Rev. Dr. H. Wilbur Skeels.

Marvin, Jameson. "The Conductor's Process." in *Five centuries of choral music: Essays in Honor of Howard Swan.* ed. Gordon Paine. Hillsdale, NY: Pendragon Press, 1988.

Slon, Michael. *Songs from the Hill: A History of the Cornell University Glee Club.* Ithaca, NY: Cornell Glee Club, 1998.

Strauch, Barbara. *The Secret Life of the Grown-Up Brain.* New York: Viking Press, 2010.

Bittman, B., L. Burk, and M. Shannon, et al. "Recreational music-making modulates the human stress response: A preliminary individualized gene expression strategy." *Medical Science Monitor* 11, no. 2, 2005.

Blood, A., and R. J. Zatorre. "Intensely pleasurable responses to music correlate with activity in brain regions implicated in reward and emotion." *Proceedings of the National Academy of Sciences* 98, no. 20, 2001.

Bungay, H., S. Clift, and A. Skingley. "The Silver Song Club Project: A sense of well-being through participatory singing." *Journal of Applied Arts and Health* 1, no. 2, 2010.

Chong, Hyun Ju. "Do we all enjoy singing? A content analysis of non-vocalists' attitudes toward singing." *The Arts in Psychotherapy* 37, no. 2, April 2010.

Chorus America. "Choral Conductors Today: A Profile." Report on Survey Findings, Chorus America, 2005.

Clift, Stephen M., and Grenville Hancox. "The Perceived Benefits of Singing: Findings from Preliminary Surveys of a University College Choral Society." *Journal of The Royal Society for the Promotion of Health* 121, no. 4, December 2001.

———. "The significance of choral singing for sustaining psychological wellbeing: findings from a survey of choristers in England, Australia and Germany," in *Music Performance Research* 3, no. 1, special issue *Music and Health,* 2010.

Clift, Stephen M., Grenville Hancox, Ian Morrison, et al. "Choral singing and psychological wellbeing: Quantitative and qualitative findings from English choirs in a cross-national survey." *Journal of Applied Arts and Health* 1, no. 1, 2010.

Davidson, Jane W., and Betty A. Bailey. "Effects of Group Singing and Performance for Marginalized and Middle-Class Singers." *Psychology of Music* 33, no. 3, July, 2005.

Durrant, Colin, and Evangelos Himonides. "What Makes People Sing Together? Socio-Psychological and Cross-Cultural Perspectives on the Choral Phenomenon." *International Journal of Music Education* os-32, November 1998.

Huron, David. "Why is sad music pleasurable? A possible role for prolactin." *Musicae Scientiae* 15, no. 2, July, 2011.

Koelsch, S., J. Fiermetz, and U. Sack, et al. "Effects of music listening on cortisol levels and propofol consumption during spinal anesthesia." *Frontiers in Psychology* 2, no. 58, 2011.

Krehbiel, H. E. "American Choral Societies and Conductors." *Harper's Weekly,* February 1, 1890.

Kreutz, Gunter, Stephan Bongard, Sonja Rohrmann, Volker Hodapp, and Dorothee Grebe. "Effects of Choir Singing or Listening on Secretory Immunoglobulin A, Cortisol, and Emotional State." *Journal of Behavioral Medicine* 27, no. 6, December 2004.

Mithin, Steven, and Lawrence D. Parsons. "Singing in the Brain." *New Scientist,* February 23, 2008.

Stefano, G. B., W. Zhu, P. Cadet, E. Salamon, and K. J. Mantione. "Music alters constitutively expressed opiate and cytokine processes in listeners." *Medical Science Monitor* 10, 2004.

Von Lob, G., P. M. Camic, and S. M. Clift. "The Use of Singing in a Group as a Response to Adverse Life Events." *International Journal of Mental Health Promotion* 12, no. 3, 2010.

Wan, Catherine Y., Theodor Rüber, Anja Hohmann, and Gottfried Schlaug. "The Therapeutic Effects of Singing in Neurological Disorders." *Music Perception* 27, no. 4, 2010.

Young, Laurel. "The Potential Health Benefits of Community Based Singing Groups for Adults with Cancer." *Canadian Journal of Music Therapy* 15, no. 1, 2009.

Zatorre, Robert J., Joyce L. Chen, and Virginia B. Penhune. "When the brain plays music: Auditory-motor interactions in music perception and production." *Nature Reviews: Neuroscience* 8, no. 7, July 2007.

Marvin, Jameson. "The Why Question: Catalyst for Inspired Teaching and Performance." Materials from lectures given at Harvard and notes for a lecture and demonstration given at Yale.

Recitative: The Chatham Street Chapel Riot

New York City Police Office Watch Return. Municipal Archives of the City of New York, master neg. 11703, roll 19.

Hewitt, John. *Protest and Progress: New York's First Black Episcopal Church Fights Racism.* Studies in African American History and Culture. New York: Garland Publishing, 2000.

Ward, Samuel Ringgold. *Autobiography of a Fugitive Negro: His Anti-Slavery Labours in the United States, Canada, and England.* London: John Snow, 1855. Digitized version at Documenting the American South, docsouth.unc.edu/neh/wards /ward.html.

"Riot at Chatham Street Chapel." Genius of Universal Emancipation, July 1834: 1, 7. Accessed via American Periodical Series Online, p. 104.

The (New-York) Sun, July 7, 1834.

New-York Evening Post, July 8, 1834.

The (New-York) Sun, July 9, 1834.

New-York Evening Post, July 10, 1834.

Niles' Weekly Register. "New York Mobs." July 19, 1834.

Frederick Douglass and Charles Lenox Remond, in *The Liberator,* July 23, 1847.

Correspondence of Jane M. Macneven to Miss Rosa P. Macneven, July 20, 1834.

Missa Simile Est Regnum Coelorum

Interviews with Prof. Stephen Clift, Canterbury Christ Church University; Jameson Marvin, emeritus director of choral activities, senior lecturer on music, Harvard University; and Dr. Noel O'Regan, University of Edinburgh.

Brown, S., M. J. Martinez, D. A. Hodges, P. T. Fox, and L. M. Parsons. "The song system of the human brain." *Cognitive Brain Research* 20, no. 3, 2004.

Buckley, Christina. "UConn Researcher: Dopamine Not About Pleasure (Anymore)." *UConn Today,* November 30, 2012.

Coleman, Daniel. *Social Intelligence: The New Science of Human Relationships.* New York: Bantam Books, 2006.

Culley, Thomas D. *Jesuits and Music . . . : A study of the musicians connected with the German College in Rome during the 17th century and of their activities in Northern Europe.* Rome: Jesuit Historical Institute, 1970; St. Louis: St. Louis University, 1970.

Jourdain, Robert. *Music, the Brain, and Ecstasy: How Music Captures Our Imagination.* New York: William Morrow & Co., 1997.

Levitin, Daniel J. *This Is Your Brain on Music.* New York: Penguin Books, 2007.

Marvin, Jameson. *The Conductor's Process from Five Centuries of Choral Music: Essays in Honor of Howard Swan.* Ed. Gordon Paine. Hillsdale, NY: Pendragon Press, 1988.

Sacks, Oliver. *Musicophilia.* New York: Alfred A. Knopf, 2008.

Storr, Anthony. *Music and the Mind.* New York: Free Press, 1992.

Chapin, Heather, Kelly Jantzen, J. A. Scott Kelso, Fred Steinberg, and Edward Large. "Dynamic Emotional and Neural Responses to Music Depend on Performance Expression and Listener Experience." Public Library of Science, *PLoS One*, December 16, 2010, www.plosone.org/article/info:doi/10.1371/journal .pone.0013812.

Cohen, Mary L. "Choral Singing and Prison Inmates: Influences of Performing in a Prison Choir." *Journal of Correctional Education* 60, no. 1, March 2009.

Davidson, Jane W., and Betty A. Bailey. "Effects of Group Singing and Performance for Marginalized and Middle-Class Singers." *Psychology of Music* 33, no. 3, July 2005.

Davidson, Jane W., and Robert Faulkner. "Men in Chorus: Collaboration and Competition in Homo-Social Vocal Behaviour." *Psychology of Music* 34, no. 2, April, 2006.

Davidson, Justin. "Measure for Measure." *The New Yorker,* August 21, 2006.

Di Pellegrino, G., L. Fadiga, L. Fogassi, V., Gallese, and G. Rizzolatti. "Understanding motor events: a neurophysiological study." *Experimental Brain Research* 91, no. 1, 1992.

Edmondson, Nelson. "An Agnostic Response to Christian Art." *Journal of Aesthetic Education* 15, no. 4, October, 1981.

Grape, C., M. Sandgren, L. O. Hansson, M. Ericson, and T. Theorell.

"Does singing promote well-being?: An empirical study of professional and amateur singers during a singing lesson." *Integrative
Physiological and Behavioral Science* 38, no. 1, Jan.–Mar. 2003.

Huron, David. "The Plural Pleasures of Music." *Proceedings of the
2004 Music and Music Science Conference,* eds. Johan Sundberg
and William Brunson. Stockholm: Kungliga Musikhögskolan
& KTH (Royal Institute of Technology), 2005.

Levitin, Daniel. "Happy Birthday iPod!" *The New York Times,*
October 22, 1011.

———. "Do You Hear What I Hear?" *The Wall Street Journal,*
December 13, 2008.

Marvin, Jameson. "Mastery of Choral Ensemble." in *Up Front! Becoming the Complete Choral Conductor,* ed. Guy B. Webb. Boston: Schirmer/ECS Publishing, 1993.

Overy, Katie, and Istvan Molnar-Szakacs. "Being Together in
Time: Musical Experience and the Mirror Neuron System."
Music Perception 26, no. 5, 2009.

Rive, Thomas N. "An Examination of Victoria's Technique of Ad-
aptation and Reworking in His Parody Masses—with Particular
Attention to Harmonic and Cadential Procedure." *Anuario musical* 24, 1969.

Rizzolatti, Giacomo. "The mirror neuron system and its function
in humans." *Anatomy and Embryology* 210, 2005. Published online by Springer Verlag, Heidelberg, October 13, 2005.

Salamone, John D., and Mercè Correa. "The Mysterious Motiva-
tional Functions of Mesolimbic Dopamine." *Neuron* 76, no. 3,
November 8, 2012.

Salimpoor, Valorie N., Mitchel Benovoy, Kevin Larcher, Alain
Dagher, and Robert J. Zatorre. "Anatomically distinct dopamine release during anticipation and experience of peak emotion
to music." *Nature Reviews: Neuroscience* 14, no. 2, February 2011.

Wan, Catherine Y., Krystal Demaine, Lauryn Zipse, Andrea

Norton, and Gottfried Schlaug. "From music making to speaking: Engaging the mirror neuron system in autism." *Brain Research Bulletin* 82, 2010.

Warren, J. D., and G. D. Schott. "Musical Hallucinations in a Musician." *Journal of Neurology*, August 2006.

Chorus America. "Choral Conductors Today." Chorus America, 2005.

Ramachandran, V. S. "The neurons that shaped civilization." TEDTalk, November 2009, ted.com.

Marvin, Jameson. "Prelude: Performing Renaissance Choral Music Today" and "The Why Question: Catalyst for Inspired Teaching and Performance." Materials from lectures given at Harvard and notes for a lecture/demonstration given at Yale.

The Last Invocation *and* Memoranda

Interview with Carl B. Schmidt, professor of music history and literature, Towson University.

Randall Thompson Papers, 85M-70 box 7, Arthur Foote folder. Houghton Library, Harvard University.

Benser, Caroline Cepin, and David Francis Urrows. *Randall Thompson: A Bio-Bibliography*. Westport, CT: Greenwood Press, 1991.
Forbes, Elliot. A History of Music at Harvard to 1972. Cambridge, MA: Department of Music, Harvard University, 1988.
Mann, Alfred, ed. *Randall Thompson: A Choral Legacy*. Boston: E. C. Schirmer Music Company, 1983.
Thompson, Randall. "Writing for the Amateur Chorus: A Chance and a Challenge." *American Choral Review* 22, no. 2; April, 1980.

Krehbiel, H. E. "American Choral Societies and Conductors." *Harper's Weekly,* February 1, 1890.

Recitative: Francis Boott and Robert Nathaniel Dett

Harvard College Library, Harvard University Archives.

Interviews with Hope Williams, great-granddaughter of Francis Boott; Brainerd Blyden-Taylor, founder, artistic director, and conductor of The Nathaniel Dett Chorale; and Dr. Bernard Kreger,secretary of the Harvard Glee Club Foundation.

Boott, Francis. *Recollections of Francis Boott.* Boston: Southgate Press, T. W. Ripley Co., 1912.
Dray, Philip. *At the Hands of Persons Unknown: The Lynching of Black America.* New York: Random House, 2002.
Dubois, W. E. B. *The Souls of Black Folk.* Chicago: A. C. McClurg & Co., 1903.
Krehbiel, Henry Edward. *Notes on the Cultivation of Choral Music and the Oratorio Society of New York.* New York: AMS Press, 1884.
McBrier, Vivian Flagg. *R. Nathaniel Dett: His Life and Works, 1882–1943.* Washington: Associated Publishers, 1977.
Simpson, Anne Key. *Follow Me: The Life and Music of R. Nathaniel Dett.* Metuchen, NJ: Scarecrow Press, 1993.

Dett, R. Nathaniel. "The Emancipation of Negro Music." Bowdoin Literary Prize, Harvard University, 1920.
Toibin, Colm. "A Death, a Book, an Apartment: The Portrait of a Lady." *The Henry James Review* 30, no. 3, 2009.

"Letters of Alice James to Anne Ashburner, 1873–78: The Joy of
Engagement," (Part 1). *Resources for American Literary Study* 27,
no. 1, 2001.

"Boott No Mystery." *Boston Sunday Herald*, May 8, 1949.
"Dett Asks Writers To Be Optimistic." *The Chicago Defender*,
March 2, 1940.

James, William. "Francis Boott: The Loving Tribute of a Friend."
Memorial address, Harvard Chapel, May 8, 1904.

O Magnum Mysterium

Interviews with Morten Lauridsen and Paul Salamunovich, music
director emeritus of the Los Angeles Master Chorale.

"Deep in the Desert, Monks Make Transcendant Music." *Weekend
Edition,* National Public Radio, May 27, 2012.
Wine, Tom, ed. *Composers on composing for choir*. Chicago:
GIA Publications, Inc., 2007.

Lauridsen, Morten. "The stories behind great works . . ." *Classic
FM Magazine,* 2007.
———. "It's a Still Life That Runs Deep." *The Wall Street Journal,*
February 21, 2009.

Live broadcast with Morten Lauridsen and Scott Simon. National
Public Radio, December 25, 1999.

Ye Shall Have a Song *and* Water Night
and Fate and Faith Songs

Interviews with Eric Whitacre and Britlin Losee.

Eric Whitacre interview by Sean Rafferty, BBC Radio 3, Octobere 7, 2011.

Eric Whitacre website: ericwhitacre.com.

Mann, Alfred, ed. *Randall Thompson: A Choral Legacy.* Boston: E. C. Schirmer Music Company, 1983.

Reimer, Benett. *A Philosophy of Music Education.* Saddle River, NJ: Prentice Hall, 1970.

"Writing for the Amateur Chorus: A Chance and a Challenge." *American Choral Review,* vol. 22, no. 2, April, 1980.

Davis, Hazel. "Military Wives Choir: The Improbable Story Behind the U.K.'s Top-Selling Christmas Single." www.billboard .biz, December 27, 2011.

Davidson, Jane W., and Betty A. Bailey; "Effects of Group Singing and Performance for Marginalized and Middle-Class Singers." *Psychology of Music* 33, no. 3, July 2005.

Grape, C., M. Sandgren, L. O. Hansson, M. Ericson, and T. Theorell. "Does singing promote well-being? An empirical study of professional and amateur singers during a singing lesson." *Integrative Physiological and Behavioral Science* 38, no. 1, 2003.

Krehbiel, H. E. "American Choral Societies and Conductors." *Harper's Weekly,* February 1, 1890.

"New look at the NEA's Survey of Public Participation in the Arts data reveals that 3 out of 4 Americans participate in the arts." Press release, National Endowment for the Arts, February 24, 2011.

ACKNOWLEDGMENTS

First, a special thank you to Jane Rosenman, the original editor, for her help in getting this book off the ground. I'm very grateful to Bonnie Recca, the Chair of the Archives Committee of Grace Church, who helped me research the history of singing at the church, and also to Reverend J. Donald Waring, the Rector of Grace Church, and Dr. Patrick Allen, the Organist and Master of Choristers, for their continued and all-important support for the Choral Society of Grace Church. I would also like to thank Harvard College/Houghton Library curators Rachel Howarth and Christina Davis (who is also a former Choral Society member), and Dr. Carl B. Schmidt, for their help with the Randall Thompson sections.

I'm extremely thankful to composers Morten Lauridsen, Eric Whitacre, and Britlin Losee, for agreeing to try to put into words what they had already put into music.

I owe a great debt to the people who read this book repeatedly, because let's face it, even if you love a book that's got to be . . . a challenge. Those people are my editor Amy Gash, my agent Betsy Lerner, and my friend Howard Mittelmark. I don't even want to think about what this book would have been like without all of you. (A few pages about singing and the rest about what a loser I am.)

I want to most warmly and sincerely thank John Maclay, who answered countless questions over two years, and explained any musical term or concept I didn't understand; former associate conductor Dylan Chan and current associate conductor Tony Bellomy, who were also patient and giving; and all the members of the Choral Society who shared their personal choral history.

Finally, to all the conductors, associate conductors, and members of the Choral Society past and present, thank you for contributing your voices to the weekly congregation where to one degree or another, sorrow is redressed and joy restored. How miraculous is that?

Stacy Horn, whom Mary Roach has hailed for "combining awe-fueled curiosity with topflight reporting skills," is the author of five nonfiction books. Horn has also contributed pieces to National Public Radio's *All Things Considered,* including the story of five West Virginia children who went missing in 1945, a story about the Vatican's search for a patron saint of the Internet, and an overview of cold-case investigation in the United States. She is the founder of the New York City–based social network Echo. Echo was home to many online media firsts, including the first interactive TV show, coproduced with the then SciFi Channel. She lives and sings in New York. Her website is www.stacyhorn.com, and the website for the Choral Society of Grace Church is www.thechoralsociety.org.